## Prelude

*Clyde v Airdrie...29th of April 1972...last game ~~~~~~~~~ 'n to avoid relegation...Billy Beattie is sent ~ ~ ~~~~~~~~~~~~~ der goes into Roddy McKenzie's arms ar. ~~~~~~~~~~~~~~~~ ·h keeps a clean sheet in his final game ~~~~~~~~~~~~~ ~ 0-0 draw means relegation for the Buk.*

## Disclaimer                              The Authors

There will be mistakes in this book – but they are not all of our making. For instance, the match programme states that Jimmy Burns made his first competitive appearance against Queen of the South. Other sources have his first appearance coming against Forfar, in the game before the QoS game. Without an absolute definitive source, we have to make a decision, rightly or wrongly. There are a few other examples of this sort of thing, where verification would take a forensic scientist and a lawyer to (perhaps) resolve the matter.

For any errors entirely attributable to ourselves please forgive us!

# Introduction

So why Season 72/73?

Well, from a personal perspective it was my first complete season following the fortunes of the Bully Wee, so everything in football and around it was new, and perhaps more importantly, interesting, to an eight-year-old boy. With no internet, and social media being confined to playground discussions about the weekend games, the match programme provided much of the news around the club, and through reading that classic work my deeper interest in the club slowly began to develop.

There was also the traditional West of Scotland visit to the relatives, where, as a mere youngster, you would often be expected to "entertain" your aunties, uncles and even big cousins with your "party piece". Not being at all interested in the performing arts, mine was honed down to reciting the Clyde team of the day…Cairney, Anderson, Swan, Burns, McVie, Ahern, Sullivan, Beattie, Millar, McGrain and Boyle substitute Hulston (and don't forget substitute Hulston) as quickly as I could, then making a fast exit!

If you read the Clyde FC Centenary Book, there is a small section in there covering the last game of season 71/72, which I touched on in "The Prelude". A small boy, seated on the wall of the "Stand" enclosure crying, is told by his dad not to worry, "because everything will be alright next season, we'll win lots of games and be back among the big boys soon".

That wee boy, whoever he was, wasn't the only one in tears; Midfielder Danny McGrain (pictured) openly displayed his emotions as he left the pitch after the match against Airdrie.

That wee boy in tears could have been any number of wee boys, including me (aside from the fact that I was in the terracing!). But the advice probably given by quite a few dad's in the ground that day, including mine, was absolutely correct. Archie Robertson assembled a team of (mainly) youngsters, appointed the youngest captain in Scottish senior football, got his team playing a method-based football that many perceive to be years ahead of its time, and got us "back up amongst the big boys" in just one season.

So, following on from "Unsung Heroes", the story of the 1966/67 season, aside from the above reasons it seemed logical to look at the next landmark in the club's history (ignoring the relegation at the end of season 71/72 of course). And since I had only attended a relatively small number of the games at Shawfield (and not forgetting my Hampden debut), and my memories as an 8-year-old can be a bit hazy, I enlisted the assistance of some Clyde supporters who were actually at most of the games, with the additional benefit that they can – more easily than I – bring personal memories and anecdotes into their writing; Alan "Aldo" Maxwell, Jim Hutchison and Graeme "Sharkey" Clark. To these guys I am indebted for their patience and willingness to give up large chunks of their personal time to submit many of the words you will read in this book.

But before I get carried away and forget to stop, let's head forward (or back) to August 1972...

Gordon Sydney

# Pre-Season Review                    Jim Hutchison

After the bitter disappointment of being relegated the previous season big changes were happening in the squad, which would take their bow at Shawfield in the friendly against English Fourth Division side Barrow.

As I vividly recall it was not with any great sense of optimism that many Clyde supporters attended the match, although, as with all football supporters, hope springs eternal at the beginning of any season. The lead-in to this particular season had been beset with problems, and a good deal of gloom still pervaded Shawfield from the previous season, following the list of players retiring or being released.

Joe McBride, a legendary figure in the history of Scottish football goalscoring forwards, decided to retire following a cartilage operation. The list of those released also included some great servants and much-loved faces, prime amongst them long-serving custodian Tommy McCulloch, who had joined the club back in the late fifties and who had won a Scottish Cup Winners medal in the victorious Clyde side of 1958.

Also leaving would be Sam Hastings, a wonderfully entertaining winger once described to me in my youth as the "Shawfield Musketeer". When I queried as to why he was called that the reply came back that he was "The Dark Tan Yin", referring to Sam's prevalence to return after the close season sporting a deep sun-tanned complexion. The great Eddie Mulheron had departed in February, a couple of months before the season end, and yet another fine servant of that era, former captain Harry Glasgow, also left the club, although he would come back to haunt us later in the season with his new club Stenhousemuir. Further casualties of the drastic reductions in our squad were goalkeeper John Wright, a fine understudy to Tommy McCulloch, Millar Hay, John McColligan, Alan Brown and John MacDonald – in total more than a third of the playing staff had gone.

Added to this, Clyde were in the midst of a player revolt that saw Johnny Flanagan, whom we had purchased at a cost of £10,000 from Partick Thistle two years previously, immediately transfer-listed. Veterans John McHugh, club captain at the time, Jim Burns and Billy Hulston – who was our top scorer in 71/72 - were also suspended by the club during the wages dispute. Both Flanagan and Hulston would be gone before the season was very old with, ironically, Hulston going to Airdrie, the club who had drawn with us at Shawfield on the last day of the previous season and effectively relegated Clyde to the Second Division.

The summation of all this turmoil was that Clyde had only fourteen signed players before this friendly, with only eight days before the season started properly with an opening League Cup tie against First Division Motherwell. So perhaps lack of optimism amongst the support can be understood, although it would prove to be unfounded in the long run.

# The 1972-73 squad
## in alphabetical order

| Player | Date of Signing | Previous Club | Occupation |
|---|---|---|---|
| Ahern, B. | Apr. '71 | Glencairn | Clerk |
| Anderson, E. | Aug. '69 | Kirkintilloch Rob Roy | P.O. Electrician |
| Beattie, W. | Aug. '69 | Baillieston | Motor Mechanic |
| Boyle, P. | Aug. '72 | Larkhall Thistle | Junior Chemist |
| Burns, J. | Feb. '68 | Cowdenbeath | Joiner |
| Cairney, J. | Oct. '71 | Coatbridge St Pat's H.S. | P.E. Student |
| Flanagan, J. | Oct. '70 | Partick Thistle | Taxi Driver |
| Houston, L. | Aug. '71 | Vale of Leven | Mechanic |
| Hulston, B. | Mar. '69 | East Stirling | Joiner |
| McGoldrick, J. | Oct. '69 | Glenboig Sports Club | Student |
| McGrain, D. | Aug. '70 | Blantyre Vics | Engineer |
| McHugh, J. | Aug. '61 | Dennistoun Waverley | Systems Analyst |
| McVie, W. | Apr. '69 | Lesmahagow | Plumber |
| Miller, S. | Oct. '70 | Glencairn | Student |
| Sullivan, D. | Aug. '70 | St Roch's | Rents Collection Dept., Glasgow Corporation |
| Swan, A. | Jan. '70 | Shettleston | Electrician |
| Thomson, C. | Nov. '70 | Kirkintilloch Rob Roy | Chauffeur |

| | |
|---|---|
| **DATE** | Friday 4th August 1972 |
| **TOURNAMENT** | Pre-season Friendly Match |
| **FINAL SCORE** | Clyde 4 Barrow 0 |
| **TEAM** | *Cairney, Anderson, Swan; McGrain, McVie, McGoldrick; Sullivan, McGuinness, Millar, Ahern and Trialist. Subs Beattie, Thomson* |
| **SCORER(S)** | *McGuinness, Boyle (2), Sullivan* |
| **REPORTER** | Jim Hutchison |

To describe the Clyde team as "a youthful side" would be an understatement, given the average age of that Clyde team was 21. Very young in the 1970's for a senior side indeed - a lot of so-called Junior sides had a much higher average age. And note that two substitutes were listed by agreement between the sides, although only one would be allowed for competitive matches, and the "trialist" turned out to be a certain Peter Boyle of which more later.

So how would these "weans" do then against the English side? Admittedly not the strongest opposition we had ever faced from South of the Border, but we weren't in great shape either judging by the pre-season "shenanigans"!

Well, to answer my own question above, "rather well" was the answer, as we thumped in four without reply. Eddie McGuinness and Dom Sullivan both scored in an emphatic victory, with Eddie opening the scoring from a Dom Sullivan cross and Dom himself rounding of a fine display by adding the fourth.

Between these goals our "trialist" from Junior side Larkhall Thistle, Peter Boyle, scored Clyde's second before half time. He repeated the feat early in the second half with Clyde's third goal, before being substituted with around fifteen minutes to go by Colin Thompson. He left the field to a rousing reception from the Clyde faithful, who were rewarded very shortly after the match with some good news.

Peter had played both his first and last match as a "trialist" for the Bully Wee, because before he left the Old Academy of Soccer and Football Science (aka Shawfield) he had put pen to paper and signed for the Bully Wee. Interestingly, Peter was instantly transformed into one of our more "experienced" players, given he was 22 after all!

Dom Sullivan was moved from his normal berth at outside right to a more inside position – what we now know as midfield – for this game, and was interviewed for the match programme afterwards...

*"My first few games for the club were at inside right, then it was out to the wing - and there I stayed. But I much prefer [my new] role. I found when I was playing on the wing, if the ball wasn't coming out to me, I was tending to let my concentration slip. But now I'm chasing back and forth – and enjoying it."*

Dom also took the opportunity to make a bold prediction..." *we really moved the ball about well against Barrow, and if we can keep up this sort of form, there's no reason at all why we can't come straight back up as champions.*"

So, a great 4-0 win in this friendly, but how would that translate when the serious stuff started? We would have to wait and see but it certainly couldn't have done the young team's confidence any harm.

# The Clyde Men of 1972-73

The Clyde squad faces the camera, back row (left to right) — Eddie Anderson, Joe McGoldrick, Willie McVie, Phil Cairney, Liam Houston, Brian Ahern, Allan Swan.
Front row (left to right) — Sam Miller, Eddie McGuinness, Peter Boyle, Danny McGrain (club captain), Colin Thomson, Dom Sullivan, Physiotherapist Lawrie Smith.
Photo by courtesy of Charles R. McBain.

## Player Pic – Peter Boyle                    Gordon Sydney

Peter Boyle holds the unofficial title of "My First Footballing Hero", given (a) that he played for the Bully Wee, and (b) he could score goals! What wouldn't we give for a wee bit of film of Peter in action for the Bully Wee?

Off the field Peter was, by all accounts, a brilliant guy, but on the park the impression I get is of someone determined to do their utmost. Extremely focused, so much so that preference would be to play in the same team as Peter, rather than play for the opponents. Not much wrong with that winning mentality though, especially as he played for the Bully Wee!

He also had a tactic of standing in front of the goalkeeper when the keeper was taking a kick-out from hand, and thumping his chest. On occasion this tactic proved utterly successful, and I'm sure I remember it resulting in a goal or very nearly a goal against Stirling Albion at Shawfield – and I'm told that wasn't the only time that happened.

But Peter was far from a "one-trick pony". Take the New Year derby game against Queens Park for instance. Peter's two goals that day were delivered via a cracking shot from well outside the penalty area, and a tap-in after he went through and rounded the keeper.

To end season 72/73, Peter's first season in the senior ranks, as top scorer with 16 goals was a tremendous feat. As if to prove it wasn't a fluke, the following season in Division One Peter scored 15 goals!

Clyde were Peter's only senior Scottish club, because his next big move was to Australia. He performed to such an extent in that country that he was "capped" for the national team against Czechoslovakia.

Peter Boyle. Born Larkhall 24 March 1951, died in Australia 18 January 2013

| | |
|---|---|
| **DATE** | Saturday 12th August 1972 |
| **TOURNAMENT** | League Cup Section 7 |
| **FINAL SCORE** | Clyde 2 Motherwell 2 |
| **TEAM** | *Cairney, Anderson, Swan; Houston, McVie, Ahern;* |
| | *Sullivan, McGuinness, Millar, McGrain and Boyle Sub* |
| | *McGoldrick* |
| **SCORER(S)** | *McVie, Sullivan* |
| **ATTENDANCE** | 2239 |
| **REPORTER** | Jim Hutchison |

At last the "real" football was back!

No more talk of huge reductions in the squad - although the "four-player-pay-rebellion" situation rumbled on – this was back to the real deal!

The friendly against Barrow had given the support a first look at Archie Robertson's new youthful side and the impressive new signing Peter Boyle, but could they "hack it" in the competitive football scene and against First Division opponents Motherwell?

After the traumatic ending to the previous season when, as a young Clyde fan, I felt the world had ended due to our relegation (a matter that, with the benefit of hindsight and maturity, I now fully realise doesn't compare with some of the other things currently happening in the world)! I also feared, like many others, that Clyde might not resurface as a side fit to compete with First Division sides again.

The match itself started, in truth, as a gritty but less-than-inspiring match for the fans at least, and while Clyde matched their First Division opponents it was no real surprise that the teams left the pitch at half time all square at 0-0.

Pre-match, Archie Robertson had promised "we will attack", and Clyde were definitely playing the better football in the second half, and on the hour mark Brian Ahern unleashed a fierce drive that brought the best out of Well's veteran keeper Billy Ritchie, at the expense of a corner. Brian gathered the ball, took the resultant corner himself, and big Willie McVie rose and met the corner to arrow a tremendous header past Ritchie and give the Bully Wee a richly deserved lead.

Clyde started to play some sweet stuff after this boost and the quality of football would, long after the game, be the main topic of conversation.

If Clyde's first goal had the home fans cheering our brilliant second goal in the 78th minute sent them into raptures. Danny McGrain, who was immense all game and reveling in his new role as Captain, won and held the ball in midfield. He spotted Dom Sullivan's clever run through and sent an inch perfect pass into his path. Dom took two strides and unleashed an unstoppable volley from the edge of the 18-yard box on the angle that flashed past the helpless Ritchie in the Motherwell goal.

Less than a minute later, though, The Shawfield Babes were given a warning when John Goldthorpe struck the base of Phil Cairney's post with the keeper beaten. It was, though, a combination of a lack of experience and a couple of moments of genius from Motherwell's little Irish winger Billy Campbell that denied Clyde both points from this opening encounter, as Kirkie Lawson headed home his crosses in the 82nd and 86th minutes.

Under normal circumstances the supporters may have been downhearted but in all honesty, whilst clearly disappointing to lose two late goals, the spirit of the side and quality of play was in such stark contrast to the previous season that the home fans left mightily encouraged by this display. Indeed, if this match was a pointer to the rest of the season, then there should have been a stampede to the bookmakers to back Clyde to make a quick return to the First Division!

## Player Pic – Phil Cairney                    Graeme Clark

Phil Cairney was one of my first Clyde heroes, capable of some truly outstanding goalkeeping but also the odd moment of madness. Indeed, everything you wanted from a goalie!

Born in 1952, Phil signed for Clyde in 1971 from Dumbarton St Pats. A Physical Education student at Jordanhill, he almost slipped through the net. Originally asked to train with Clyde in the summer of 1970, he did not return to Shawfield as he felt, with the new season starting, he "was in the way". Luckily, after a couple of weeks, Clyde got back in touch with him to ask where he was and the rest, as they say, is history, and he signed professional forms the following year.

In his first season, 1971-72, Phil was in and out of the team, unable to find a consistent level of performance, but with the legendary Tommy McCulloch being released at the end of that season, 1972-73 saw him start the season as first choice 'keeper. In fact, incredible as it seems now, he was our only signed 'keeper.

He was not particularly tall for a goalkeeper, standing 5' 11", but he was agile, had great reflexes and was capable of outstanding shot-stopping. Described during the season as demonstrating "poise, precision and near perfection", his league record over the season bore witness to this – just 20 goals conceded in 32 league matches. He missed 4 games through injury, towards the end of the season, in which we conceded 6 goals, which served to emphasise what an important player he was for Clyde, with his ability to stay "switched on" during the many games in which Clyde were largely dominant, and in which for large parts he was a virtual bystander.

Phil was with Clyde until 1977, posting 145 appearances for the Bully Wee, before signing for East Stirling, where he remained until 1979. As well as Clyde legend, his other claim to fame is that he is the nephew of the famous Scottish actor John Cairney, and in fact (almost!) appeared on the cover of a book written by his Uncle, "The Sevenpenny Gate", facing a penalty taken by John.

## And in the red corner...

Cock-a-hoop with his goal against Motherwell, only his fourth for the Bully Wee, Willie McVie revealed in an interview for the "Official Match day Programme" that he had "*a small sidestake on with Danny McGrain which says I will score more goals then he will this season...and I've no intention of losing my money.*"

Both players had managed three goals apiece for the Bully Wee the previous season, so a close contest was expected (if you don't know the result you can always jump to the end of the book)!

*Latest score...Willie edges ahead...Willie McVie 1 Danny McGrain 0*

## Danny as Captain...

Danny might have dropped behind in his goalscoring contest with Willie, but he could always remind him who was Captain! In an interview for the Match Programme, Danny McGrain, recalls being made captain for the pre-season friendly against Barrow...

"*I was told of my appointment about ten minutes before the friendly game against Barrow*", said Danny, and "*at that stage I thought it was just a temporary thing since last season's skipper Jim Burns was unavailable. Now I'm quite happy, we're all responding and my ambition now is to lead Clyde to a Second Division Championship.*"

| DATE | Wednesday 16th August 1972 |
|------|---------------------------|
| **TOURNAMENT** | League Cup Section 7 |
| **FINAL SCORE** | Dundee 2 Clyde 1 |
| ***TEAM*** | ***Cairney, Anderson, Swan; Houston, McVie, Ahern; Sullivan, McGuinness, Millar, McGrain and Boyle Sub McGoldrick*** |
| **SCORER(S)** | ***Boyle*** |
| **ATTENDANCE** | 4868 |
| **REPORTER** | Graeme Clark |

After their fine performance in their first League Cup game against First Division Motherwell, an unchanged Clyde headed to Dens Park to face a Dundee team who had scored EIGHT in their opening game away to East Stirling, with danger man John Duncan accounting for FIVE of those goals.

A good crowd of around 4,900 watched as Dundee took advantage of the strong wind at their back to force the pace in the first half, and at times it looked as though they would overwhelm their Second Division opponents. But Clyde did fashion some chances, and indeed spurned two early opportunities when first Sam Millar then Brian Ahern were denied by the home defence. Sam Millar also hit woodwork, but generally the early part of the first half was mostly one-way traffic towards the Clyde goal, albeit with Phil Cairney in inspired form. Phil, though, had to admit defeat in the 20th minute when that man Duncan netted with a far post header from a Jocky Scott free kick.

The remainder of the first half generally provided more chances, including two strong penalty claims, for the home side, who were by now dominating the game, but Clyde reached the interval trailing by just that one goal.

Clyde burst out of the traps at the start of the second half, taking advantage of the wind which was now at their backs, to such an extent that it was no great surprise when they grabbed an equaliser. Eddie McGuinness met a Dom Sullivan corner at the near post, knocking the ball to the back post where Peter Boyle made no mistake with a close-range header.

However, parity did not last long – how often down through the years have we seen that – and Dundee restored their lead within two minutes. Jocky Scott was again the provider, and this time his namesake Ian got the vital last touch.

13

The latter stages of the game were fairly equal with both teams creating chances. Phil Cairney continued to enhance his reputation with some great goalkeeping, including one outstanding stop from Jimmy Wilson, but it was Clyde who were to have the last chance when Alan Swan fired inches over with just two minutes to go.

Overall then a deserved win for a very useful Dundee side, who would go on to win this group winning all 6 games, scoring 19 goals in the process. But Clyde emerged with great credit for a battling performance, not short of skill, that augured well for the league campaign ahead.

Eddie Anderson, in an interview for the match programme around this time, stated, *"I'm still confident – and I know the rest of the side agree with me – that we can come back up in one season."*

| | |
|---|---|
| **DATE** | Saturday 19th August 1972 |
| **TOURNAMENT** | League Cup Section 7 |
| **FINAL SCORE** | Clyde 3 East Stirling 1 |
| ***TEAM*** | ***Cairney, Anderson, Swan; Houston, McVie, Ahern; Sullivan, McGuinness, Millar, McGrain and Boyle Sub McGoldrick*** |
| **SCORER(S)** | ***Boyle, Millar, Sullivan*** |
| **ATTENDANCE** | 1221 |
| **REPORTER** | Graeme Clark |

With just a point from their opening two League Cup matches, albeit against higher league opposition, this was a match Clyde had to win, and of course it presented an opportunity to consider how we might fare in the lower league this season. The only change in the line-up was Colin Thomson being drafted in as a direct replacement for Eddie McGuinness.

East Stirling had lost both their opening fixtures, conceding nine goals along the way, despite the presence of former Clyde player Jim McGregor in the centre of their defence.

In front of 1,200 fans, Clyde started strongly, and were dismayed when a goal by Peter Boyle was chalked off for an offside offence against Sam Millar after only two minutes.

The disappointment was not to linger for long however, because a matter of minutes later Sam headed home a cross from Dom Sullivan, who was to have a hand in all three Clyde goals. As sometimes happens, Clyde seemed to lose their way a wee bit after this and East Stirling applied a fair bit of pressure on the Clyde goal, with Phil Cairney having to produce a smart stop to prevent Davie Robertson from scoring. Willie McVie then earned the applause of the home support with a goal-saving tackle on Dougie George, who looked on the point of breaking through the Clyde defence.

East Stirling had come right back into the game, and if truth be told were deserving of a goal. It duly arrived in the 16th minute when Ian Browning prodded home a low cross by Dougie George. Clyde were clearly stung by this and they in turn started to dominate the visitors, whose cause was not helped when goalkeeper Archibald had to go off injured, to be replaced by defender Gordon Simpson.

In 31 minutes, Clyde's second goal duly arrived when Sullivan's fierce drive thundered off the bar and Sam Millar was handily placed to knock in the rebound. Half time came with Clyde now well in command, but only holding a single goal advantage.

Clyde started the second half where they left off in the first. Chances came and went, with Alan Swan and Colin Thompson missing early opportunities. East Stirling too had the occasional chance, and Phil Cairney had to remain alert in the Clyde goal, however the decisive third goal finally came in the 73rd minute, another piledriver from Man-of-the-Match Dom Sullivan finding the net this time.

The remainder of the match, with victory all but won, saw Clyde relax and play some delightful football, although Manager Robertson bemoaned the fact that victory had not been secured earlier than it was. Overall, Clyde were by far the better side, and deserved the victory, playing with a fluency that their opponents could not match. This win saw Clyde move into second top position in the League Cup section 7.

"*We stumbled a bit at times*," said manager Archie Robertson. "*Our play was looking very fluent, then for no apparent reason, it would become hesitant. But for all that, we dominated the major part of the game and created quite a number of good chances.*"

A local journalist was a bit more fulsome in his praise...

"*Clyde kept to their word on Saturday and served up one of the most exciting displays of attacking football Shawfield has ever seen...Boyle and Millar were outstanding, and Dom Sullivan had one of his best games ever...*"

Heady stuff indeed!

| | |
|---|---|
| **DATE** | Wednesday 23rd August 1972 |
| **TOURNAMENT** | League Cup Section 7 |
| **FINAL SCORE:** | Clyde 0 Dundee 1 |
| **TEAM** | *Cairney, Anderson, Swan; Houston, McVie, Ahern; Sullivan, McGuinness, Millar, McGrain and Boyle Sub Beattie (for McGuinness)* |
| **ATTENDANCE** | 1580 |
| **REPORTER**: | Gordon Sydney |

The old saying "Football can be a funny old game" was possibly never more truly illustrated than in this game. Dundee were the current leaders in our League Cup section had a 100% record, and they were joint-top goal scorers in the League Cup. The almost-ubiquitous connection with the Bully Wee was provided in the shape of Dundee manager Davie White (pictured), who had steered the club through that remarkable 66/67 season, just five years previous.

Right from the start Clyde took the game to the Dark Blues. Doug Houston headed the ball out for a corner just as Brian Ahern's superb cross was about to fall for Eddie McGuinness; Thomson Allan pulled off a great save from an Eddie Anderson shot; then a Dom Sullivan shot skimmed the crossbar.

Midway through the first half, when all was looking positive from a Clyde perspective, disaster struck. Dom Sullivan and Eddie McGuinness inadvertently bumped into each other, Iain Philip took the ball, played a one-two with Bobby Wilson, and fired a wicked shot past Phil Cairney.

Still the Bully Wee fought like terriers. Alan Swan's rocket from 30 yards crashed off the bar, and another Brian Ahern cross was scythed wildly over his own crossbar by Ian Scott. The introduction of Billy Beattie for Eddie McGuinness gave no respite to a beleaguered Dundee defence, but there was to be no fine ending as The Dark Blues ran out narrow winners.

But despite this defeat, the Shawfield crowd stayed to applaud Archie's young team off the park - Football, as they say, can be a funny old game!

| | |
|---|---|
| **DATE** | Saturday 26<sup>th</sup> August 1972 |
| **TOURNAMENT** | League Cup Section 7 |
| **FINAL SCORE** | Motherwell 1 Clyde 1 |
| **TEAM** | *Cairney, Anderson, Swan; Houston, McVie, Ahern; Sullivan, McGuinness, Millar, McGrain and Boyle Sub Beattie* |
| **SCORER(S)** | *McGuinness* |
| **ATTENDANCE** | 4327 |
| **REPORTER:** | Alan Maxwell |

After the first four Sectional ties, the famous Bully Wee were still in with a shout of qualification from the section, even allowing for the presence of two established First Division outfits.

Having surrendered a two-goal advantage to the 'Well so late in the day in the earlier Shawfield encounter, they were determined to make their mark at Fir Park. Clyde were first to show, when Super Dom Sullivan forced a corner on the right. Unfortunately, he made a hash of the corner kick. Then Eddie Anderson, of all people, almost opened the scoring with an overlap run when his left footed lob had Billy Ritchie at full stretch to tip the ball over for a corner. In 25 minutes 'Well got a penalty when Alan "Aldo" Swan whipped the feet from right-winger John Gray. All was not lost however; keeper Phil Cairney hurled himself across the goal to stop Jackie McInally's spot kick.

*Phil Cairney brilliantly saves Jackie McInally's penalty*

Moments later, and Cairney again was to prove a hero, this time dealing with a fierce drive, again from John Gray.

Clyde broke the deadlock in the 32$^{nd}$ minute. Dom Sullivan fired in a shot which hit Eddie McGuinness and stopped. McGuinness, left with a clear sight of goal, turned quickly and hit a grounder past the helpless Billy Ritchie, and into the corner of the "onion bag"! One-nil to the Bully Wee!!!

In an exciting end to the first half, 'keeper Ritchie touched over a drive from Peter Boyle, then Lawson missed an absolute sitter for the home outfit from all of two yards, allowing Eddie Anderson to boot clear from the goal-line.

The second half was to carry on in similar vein; Willie McVie tested Ritchie with a low direct free kick. Then the famous Tom Forsyth tried to catch out Cairney with a clever back header. Sadly, the inevitable equaliser had to come; with around twelve minutes to go Willie McVie failed to clear his lines, leaving centre-forward Jim McCabe with only Cairney to beat, which he did with considerable aplomb.

Dom Sullivan and skipper Danny McGrain were absolutely stand-outs against the higher League opponents. Our young skipper, though, had suffered a knock which was to render him doubtful for the forthcoming midweek fixture at Firs Park against the mighty 'Shire.

### *Dom Sullivan Fan Club*

The player said to be most embarrassed at the club was Dom Sullivan, because two young girls, regular visitors to Shawfield, had asked his permission to form the Dom Sullivan Fan Club. Apparently, *"the blushing idol is, deep down, quite thrilled at the prospect, and is at present filling in the questionnaire submitted by the girls."*

## Player Pic – Eddie McGuinness                    Alan Maxwell

Eddie was only with the club a little over a season, but fortunately for the Bully Wee, this was the season. Signed while still in his teens, he was spotted playing for Sunnybank Juveniles in his home town of Greenock. He certainly impressed, as after just one half of a trial game against Airdrie Reserves, he was persuaded to put pen to paper.

Never the quickest, Eddie did, however, prove to be a team player, and featured regularly in what used to be known as an inside-right berth. His season started brightly, indeed Eddie it was who was to bag the very first goal of the season, in the pre-season friendly at Shawfield against Barrow. He also opened the scoring against First Division Motherwell at Fir Park, just a couple of weeks later in the League Cup sectional encounter.

In many respects it would be a season of highs and lows for Eddie, who was to feature in 14 matches, but there is no doubt he contributed positively to the Championship winning side, in his first season in senior football.

Sadly, his career petered out after this, but perhaps surprisingly he was freed by the club at the end of the season. He signed for Stranraer, where he spent less than a full season before signing on at St. Mirren. From there it was on to Dunipace Juniors and an early end to what had seemed a promising career.

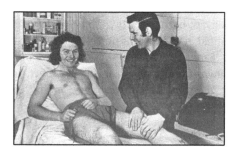

*Eddie receives treatment from Physio Lawrie Smith*

20

| | |
|---|---|
| **DATE** | Wednesday 30th August 1972 |
| **TOURNAMENT** | League Cup Section 7 |
| **FINAL SCORE** | East Stirling 0 Clyde 2 |
| **TEAM** | *Cairney, Anderson, Swan; Houston, McGoldrick, Ahern; Sullivan, McGuinness, Millar, McGrain and Boyle Sub Thomson (for McGuinness)* |
| **SCORER(S)** | *Swan, Sullivan* |
| **ATTENDANCE** | 614 |
| **REPORTER** | Gordon Sydney |

The pre-match news was that teenage Captain Danny McGrain was doubtful, due to receiving treatment for a leg injury. But being of such character, Danny played, although whether he was fully fit or not became a post-match debating point.

Regardless, the team was along the usual lines, and knew what they – and others - needed to do to qualify for the latter stages of the League Cup, namely

1.  achieve victory at Firs Park,
2.  and hope that Dundee would defeat Motherwell by a few goals.

Motherwell had scored 10 goals against Clyde's 7, and both teams had conceded 7, so a Motherwell defeat, combined with a Clyde win, could just ease Clyde into the second qualifying place in the group.

Objective One was achieved; Thirty minutes into the game full-back Alan Swan rewound the clock back to the time when he was a centre-forward, and scored from six yards.

Dom Sullivan then got our second goal just five minutes after the interval. East Stirling fought valiantly, and were seemingly denied a penalty when Joe McGoldrick tripped Billy Little in the penalty box, but it wasn't to be for the 'Shire.

Objective Two wasn't achieved, by the cruelest of methodologies in our case; goals scored. Allied with Clyde's win came the news that Motherwell had lost 1-2 to Dundee, so the final Section 7 group table looked like this...

| | P | W | D | L | F | A | Pts |
|---|---|---|---|---|---|---|---|
| Dundee | 6 | 6 | 0 | 0 | 19 | 5 | 12 |
| Motherwell | 6 | 2 | 2 | 2 | 11 | 9 | 6 |
| Clyde | 6 | 2 | 2 | 2 | 9 | 7 | 6 |
| East Stirling | 6 | 0 | 0 | 6 | 4 | 23 | 0 |

Thus, it was Motherwell who moved into the next phase of the tournament, by virtue of having scored just two more goals.

Whilst we missed out on progressing further in the League Cup, it was by the tightest of margins, and the positivity of our performances were already being noted by some journalists – "**WATCH CLYDE**" screamed one headline, with the journalist going on to say "**Clyde must be disappointed at not qualifying...they're a young side – average age around 20 – and they'll come good**."

Meanwhile, Chairman Willie Dunn issued a message of "***Thanks!***" to the fans…

"***Your enthusiasm was of the greatest help to the players, and they have expressed their thanks. Their obvious new urge and confidence will be helped greatly by a continuance of this type of support.***"

| | |
|---|---|
| **DATE** | Saturday 2nd September 1972 |
| **TOURNAMENT** | League Division Two |
| **FINAL SCORE** | Montrose 0 Clyde 1 |
| **TEAM** | *Cairney, Anderson, Swan; Houston, McGoldrick, Ahern; Sullivan, McGuinness, Millar, McGrain and Boyle Sub Thomson* |
| **SCORER(S)** | *Boyle* |
| **ATTENDANCE** | 1285 |
| **REPORTER** | Jim Hutchison |

The Clyde pay dispute had come to an end during the week prior to this match, with Jim Burns and Billy Hulston returning to training, joining John McHugh who had re-signed earlier. Midfielder Burns and striker Hulston had not re-signed yet but it had seemed likely they would come into line.

Due to missing several weeks training none of them realistically could be expected to be selected, so Clyde would have to begin their league campaign by putting their faith in youth in their efforts to gain promotion back to the First Division.

Both Burns and McHugh would play their part this season but Billy Hulston would head to Airdrie (where he scored the winner v Celtic in his first match); the other "pay rebel" John Flanagan sadly never played senior football again, eventually going into the junior football ranks with St Rochs.

Clyde, as we have seen, were very unfortunate not to qualify from their League Cup Section; Montrose, on the other hand, had finished bottom of their section having conceded 16 goals in the six sectional ties. Manager Alex Stuart, not unsurprisingly, made wholesale changes for the visit of Clyde in this curtain-raiser for the 1972-73 league season. One interesting approach by Alex was to switch his skipper Ian Thompson to right back to try to nullify livewire Peter Boyle, who was already getting a lot of good press since coming in to the Bully Wee's first team.

Another tactic that became apparent right from the start that was that Montrose had set their stall out for a draw (or as modern parlance would have it, they "parked the bus"), and it certainly worked for the first half at least, as the teams turned around goalless.

In the second half Clyde were so far on top that Phil Cairney in the visiting goal could have had a seat in the crowd (or maybe on the aforementioned bus)! Indeed, he must have felt quite lonely at times as Montrose sat so deep that Eddie Anderson and Alan Swan were effectively acting as wingers!

Seriously, it was as well Phil was there though, as later on he produced a great save from Gordon Crammond, the wee Montrose winger. Only Crammond and Brian Third offered anything going forward from a dour, defensive home side.

For Clyde, Brian Ahern was having probably his best game of the season and was pulling all the strings in midfield, prompting and prodding trying to crack the Montrose defence, and eventually Clyde found a way through, although it took us to the 74th minute. With the Montrose defenders looking for an offside flag or the ref's whistle, nippy winger Peter Boyle ran through and placed the ball wide of the wonderfully named [George] Whisker (surely as a goalkeeper his nickname must have been "The Cat") and into the net for the only goal of the match.

| | P | W | L | D | Pt |
|---|---|---|---|---|---|
| Cowdenbeath | 2 | 2 | 0 | 0 | 4 |
| St Mirren | 2 | 2 | 0 | 0 | 4 |
| Stirling Alb. | 2 | 2 | 0 | 0 | 4 |
| Queen of South | 2 | 2 | 0 | 0 | 4 |
| Forfar Ath. | 2 | 1 | 0 | 1 | 3 |
| Raith Rov. | 1 | 1 | 0 | 0 | 2 |
| Alloa Ath. | 1 | 1 | 0 | 0 | 2 |
| **Clyde** | **1** | **1** | **0** | **0** | **2** |
| Hamilton | 2 | 1 | 1 | 0 | 2 |
| East Stirling | 2 | 0 | 0 | 2 | 2 |
| Brechin City | 2 | 1 | 1 | 0 | 2 |
| Queen's Park | 2 | 0 | 1 | 1 | -1 |
| Dunfermline | 1 | 0 | 1 | 0 | 0 |
| Stenhousemuir | 1 | 0 | 1 | 0 | 0 |
| Albion Rov. | 1 | 0 | 1 | 0 | 0 |
| Montrose | 2 | 0 | 2 | 0 | 0 |
| Stranraer | 2 | 0 | 2 | 0 | 0 |
| Clydebank | 2 | 0 | 2 | 0 | 0 |
| Berwick R. | 2 | 0 | 2 | 0 | 0 |

As far as the travelling Clyde support were concerned Peter Boyle was the "cat's whiskers" and the "toast of the town" in several bars on the long journey home.

So, we were off and running then with two points in the bag, however early optimism was respectfully held in check by reference to that old cliché "it's not where you start but where you finish that counts".

# ClydePix                                    Gordon Sydney

During the course of the season the club ventured into the Commercial side of things more than ever before, with the main outlet for these items being the new Club Shop, opened under the Stand at Shawfield and run by Jim Moran at the time.

Various items were produced and sold, not least of which was the Clyde FC single by Fraser Bruce and the players, and there were also pennants, keyrings, and a series of pictures of the players, with space below for their autographs - ClydePix!

There are eight of these pictures in my personal collection, all of them autographed by the player with the exception of Peter Boyle, which sadly will forever remain unsigned. And, of course, they weren't black & white – they had a red border, with "ClydePix" written in white, and for finality the rear of the card was blank. They retailed for 5p each, and were issued in batches throughout the season, if I remember correctly.

## Player Pic – Danny McGrain                    Alan Maxwell

Captain courageous if ever there was one. Think Billy Bremner, Asa Hartford or Archie Gemmill, only better! Having been a bit of a hothead the previous season, gaffer Archie Robertson decided to bestow the responsibility of Captain, and boy, what a difference. Youngest club captain in Scotland, probably the smallest club captain in Scotland, our skipper was the full package. Danny took on the role like a duck to water. His aggressive midfield ball winning was a big part of the effort in supplying Sullivan and Peter Boyle in their scoring exploits.

An ever-present in the side, as Clyde cemented their Title challenge, a national newspaper referred to Danny as "the Billy Bremner of Shawfield". Thoroughly deserved praise for our wee battler who would lead the club to the Second Division Championship.

Famously pictured in tears after the Airdrie match that saw us relegated the previous season, Danny seemed to impact on most people that came into contact with him, whether on or off the park.

**Gordon Sydney** has a particular memory of Danny…" My abiding memory of Danny isn't on the park, but off it. I stayed two minutes away from him in East Kilbride at the time, and my best friend at the time and myself, sometime during the course of this season, finally plucked up enough courage to knock his door and ask him for *his* autograph (never mind the team) for my new Clyde FC Autograph book. I have no recollection as to whether or not Danny had any sort of conversation with a couple of nine-year olds at his back door, but suffice to say I am positive "leave it with me" was at least part of Danny's reply.

Filled with bravado and courage, we went back some nights later, and lo-and-behold Danny returned my autograph book, signed by the entire squad, thus ensuring at least one wee boy went to bed very happy that night!"

| DATE | Saturday 9th September 1972 |
|---|---|
| TOURNAMENT | League Division Two |
| FINAL SCORE | Clyde 1 Queens Park 1 |
| TEAM | *Cairney, Anderson, Swan; Houston, McGoldrick, Ahern; Sullivan, McGuinness, Millar, McGrain and Boyle Sub Thomson* |
| SCORER(S) | *Houston* |
| ATTENDANCE | 1594 |
| REPORTER | Graeme Clark |

Our first home League game of the season simultaneously gave us our first derby match of the season, with the visit of near-neighbours Queens Park. The displays in the League Cup, coupled with the opening day win over Montrose, had raised expectations at Shawfield.

So, what of the game? Well, ultimately it was a hard-fought stalemate with Clyde being brought back to earth with a bump, only gaining a point with a late equaliser that served to remind officials, players and fans that a tough season lay ahead and Clyde would have to battle for every point.

The game started off at a frantic pace, with Queen's keeper John Taylor pulling off a good early save from Sullivan. However, The Spiders were not content to sit back, and soon forced their way into the game. First John McGowan came close with a free kick for the Amateurs, before Bobby Morrison failed to hit the target with a simple chance, the Clyde defence being all-at-sea. As play swung from end-to-end, Eddie McGuinness headed over for Clyde from an Ahern free kick and a good chance went abegging. Danny McGrain was then given a severe lecture by referee Greenlees following a foul. From the resultant free kick, Queens had another opportunity but Ally Scott headed straight at Phil Cairney from a good position. The last chance of the half fell to the same Queens Park player, but he shot wildly over and half time arrived with the scores level.

If Archie Robertson was happy to get his team into the dressing room on level terms after the first half, so that he could regroup them and push on in the second half, he was to be disappointed. Within two minutes of the restart The Spiders were ahead, with Willie Whyte meeting a cross from Bobby Morrison to send a diving header past Phil Cairney. There followed a period of scrappy play ultimately dominated by Clyde, but punctuated with petty fouls that saw Alan Swan and Ally Scott booked after a bout of "handbags", then Peter Boyle of Clyde, and Ian Robertson of Queens were booked in separate incidents. While Clyde were generally having the better of the second half, they were struggling to make any headway against a resolute Queens team determined to hold what they had.

In an attempt to change their luck Archie Robertson made a substitution, taking off Eddie McGuinness and replacing him with Colin Thomson. It was seemingly to no avail, and Clyde continued to "huff-and-puff" looking for the equaliser. When it did eventually come it was from an unlikely source.

Dom Sullivan, who had been quiet throughout, swung a free kick into the Queens penalty area. For once, the away defence failed to clear their lines and Liam Houston emerged as Clyde's hero, stepping in to finish clinically, perhaps recalling the earlier phase in his football career when he had played as centre forward before converting to a defender.

So, all in all a hard-earned point that kept Clyde handily placed in the very early stages of the campaign.

---

The 1594 fans at this game may have thought they got a bargain with the entertainment on offer from this match, but that was maybe a wee bit away from the truth! However it happened, Clyde charged some paying customers First Division prices for this match, our first league match as a Second Division side!

To be fair, the club statement issued at the time implies that the error was noticed before kick-off, and a refund was offered to any fan who had paid the higher price.

No-one claimed the refund!

## Player Pic – Jim Burns                    Gordon Sydney

The contractual dispute by several of the more senior players at the start of season 72/73 probably cost Jim Burns a "better" placing in some record books.

After he followed Archie Robertson from Cowdenbeath, Jim went straight into the Clyde first team – and stayed there. So, from his debut on the 20th of April 1968 through to our relegation on the 29th of April 1972, Jim played in every match – an incredible total of 179 games.

With the contractual dispute, Jim missed 8 matches, then normal service was resumed, with Jim playing another 83 consecutive matches. So, if we "remove" those 8 matches, Jim played 262 consecutive matches for the Bully Wee! Regardless of the missing games, he was truly a remarkable and consistent performer.

Aside from a great level of physical fitness, maybe Jim's advantage was his versatility. Jim's footballing skills, allowing him to play in any number of positions in midfield or defence – he even deputised in goals at Ibrox on one occasion – made him a great team player.

But of course, the team's gain is the player's loss, in that he doesn't get to establish himself in a fixed position. Ultimately, being asked to play left back (not Jim's favoured position) when there was another left back at the club led to Jim's departure to Stirling Albion.

Co-incidentally, Jim's three senior clubs in his 20-year career were Cowdenbeath, Clyde and Stirling Albion – the three clubs that led the league in season 72/73.

| | |
|---|---|
| **DATE** | Tuesday 12th September 1972 |
| **TOURNAMENT** | League Division Two |
| **FINAL SCORE** | Forfar Athletic 0 Clyde 2 |
| **TEAM** | *Cairney, Anderson, Swan; Houston, Burns, Ahern; Sullivan, Thomson, Beattie, McGrain and Boyle Sub Unknown* |
| **SCORER(S)** | *Boyle (2)* |
| **ATTENDANCE** | 1085 |
| **REPORTER** | Gordon Sydney |

One of the easiest – and simultaneously hardest – match reports to write was this game, simply because there isn't a lot of information available on it. Forfar were unbeaten at home until the Bully Wee came calling. Two cracking goals from Peter Boyle ended the home record, and the team as a whole turned in a strong display.

Meanwhile, Billy Beattie gave his thoughts on our two full-backs Eddie Anderson and Alan Swan…

*"**Without a doubt, I would say we've got the best pair of young full-backs in the Second Division. Aye, even including the First Division. They can inter-change…they can move up in support of their attack…and they can make (and take) goal-scoring chances**"*

| | |
|---|---|
| **DATE** | Saturday 16<sup>th</sup> September 1972 |
| **TOURNAMENT** | League Division Two |
| **FINAL SCORE** | Queen of the South 0 Clyde 0 |
| **TEAM** | *Cairney, Anderson, Swan; Houston, Burns, Ahern; Sullivan, Thomson, Beattie, McGrain and Boyle Sub Millar* |
| **ATTENDANCE** | 2131 |
| **REPORTER** | Graeme Clark |

Queen of the South were a strong side and had started the season well, but as it transpired this was a game that Clyde ought to have won convincingly, however they just could not convert their outfield dominance into goals despite having numerous attempts throughout the ninety minutes.

In the home line-up were left back Robert Thorburn and right winger John Dempster, both of whom would play for Clyde in future years.

The impressive Queens keeper, John Lyle, was kept busy right from kick off, never more so than when denying Billy Beattie twice, first in stopping a shot from close range then, secondly, an equally impressive save from a powerful header that looked a certain goal. As half time approached, Queens were starting to find a foothold in the game but still it was a slick Clyde side on the front foot, creating the majority of chances. The away team did, however, get a shock just before the interval when Hugh McLaughlin of Queens saw his net-bound shot cleared off the line with Phil Cairney stranded.

The story of the game was much the same in the second half, with Clyde continuing to have the bulk of the play and chances. The game was being played at a blistering pace with Lyle repeatedly denying the Clyde forwards. Dom Sullivan produced some of his customary magic with a weaving run that left three defenders in his wake, but Tony Connell managed to clear for a corner before Dom could inflict damage on the home team.

In the end both sides had to be content with a share of the spoils, a result which boss Archie Robertson seemed reasonably content with

*"We played well enough to bring home the two points but failed to convert our pressure into goals. Their keeper had a brilliant game and handled everything we could throw at him"*

All in all, a decent point against a team above Clyde in the league. The result left Clyde handily placed to mount a serious challenge in the league over the forthcoming weeks but still a game that left a "what if" taste in the mouth.

### Danny McGrain – With or Without?

Early on in the season Danny shaved his beard off…

Which "Danny" do you prefer?

| | |
|---|---|
| **DATE** | Wednesday 20th September 1972 |
| **TOURNAMENT** | League Division Two |
| **FINAL SCORE** | Clyde 3 Forfar Athletic 2 |
| **TEAM** | *Cairney, Anderson, Swan; Houston, Burns, Ahern; Sullivan,* |
| | *Beattie, Millar, McGrain and Boyle Sub Hulston (for Boyle)* |
| **SCORER(S)** | *Beattie, Ahern, Hulston* |
| **ATTENDANCE** | 949 |
| **REPORTER** | Gordon Sydney |

Due to vagaries of the fixture compiler, Clyde met Forfar Athletic for the second time in eight days, this time in a home league game for the Bully Wee. Our away record was keeping us in fifth place, but that was largely because we had only played that single home (drawn) game against Queens Park. Just as in that game, a late goal against tonight's opponents, ninth-placed Forfar, was to help our cause no end...

There were only ten minutes on the clock when Eddie Anderson managed to do what Phil Cairney couldn't do – keep out a net-bound shot from Jim Finlayson. Unfortunately, Eddie had punched the ball clear, the ref correctly awarded the penalty, and Finlayson himself scored the spot-kick (thankfully indiscretions like Eddie's handball weren't punishable by an immediate sending-off back in those days).

Eddie Anderson was certainly having an eventful night thus far, and he was involved in the second goal of the night – this time at the right end! It was midfielder Billy Beattie who latched on to Eddie's through ball in the 19th minute of the first half, and crashed the ball well beyond keeper Jim Milne's reach.

But the first half certainly wasn't finished there. Six minutes from the break, when Forfar's Joe Watson crossed, John Bojczuk was in the right place to spectacularly hook his shot past Phil Cairney.

Into the second half, and Clyde managed to draw themselves level again, this time it was courtesy of Brian Ahern, who beat keeper Milne with an angled drive.

Was there any more excitement left in this match? Turns out there was. With just four minutes left on the clock, Brian Ahern's piledriver rebounded off the bar, and there was Billy Hulston – last season's top scorer and making his first appearance of the new season – to put the ball into the net and give us our first home league win of the season.

These two points left Clyde handily-placed in the chasing pack...

| | P | W | D | L | Pts |
|---|---|---|---|---|---|
| Stirling A. | 6 | 6 | 0 | 0 | 12 |
| C'denbeath | 6 | 6 | 0 | 0 | 12 |
| St Mirren | 6 | 4 | 0 | 2 | 8 |
| **Clyde** | **5** | **3** | **2** | **0** | **8** |
| Raith R. | 5 | 3 | 1 | 1 | 7 |
| Albion R. | 5 | 3 | 1 | 1 | 7 |
| Q.o.S. | 6 | 3 | 1 | 2 | 7 |
| Dunfermline | 5 | 3 | 0 | 2 | 6 |
| Alloa | 4 | 2 | 1 | 1 | 5 |
| Hamilton | 6 | 2 | 1 | 3 | 5 |
| Forfar A. | 6 | 2 | 1 | 3 | 5 |
| Montrose | 5 | 2 | 0 | 3 | 4 |
| E. Stirling | 6 | 1 | 2 | 3 | 4 |
| Jueen's Park | 6 | 1 | 2 | 3 | 4 |
| Stenh's'muir | 4 | 1 | 1 | 2 | 3 |
| Stranraer | 4 | 1 | 0 | 3 | 2 |
| Brechin C. | 6 | 1 | 0 | 5 | 2 |
| Clydebank* | 6 | 0 | 1 | 5 | 1 |
| Berwick R. | 5 | 0 | 0 | 5 | 0 |

## Player Pic – Billy Hulston          Gordon Sydney

As soon as Harry Hood moved to Celtic in mid-March 1969, Clyde splashed out some £10000 of the fee received from Celtic on signing Billy Hulston from East Stirling. Billy had attracted attention as a goal scoring inside-forward of some repute for East Stirling, so Clyde gave him the chance to make the journey from Firs Park to Shawfield, and from Second to First Division football. Standing at 5' 10", and weighing in around 11st 5lbs, his experience and ability as both goalscorer and creator of chances stood both him and Clyde in good stead, and he formed an effective partnership with Johnny Flanagan after he moved from Partick Thistle in October 1970. Billy finished top scorer for the club in each of the three full seasons he was with the club, including 71/72, when we were relegated.

His contribution in season 72/73 didn't start immediately, because he was one of the senior players involved in a contractual dispute at the start of the season. When his season finally got underway, his contribution was to be mostly from the bench as youth came to the fore. Statistics will show that whilst he only started one game, he was on the bench in at least a dozen other games that season, and he chipped in with two goals.

A move to Airdrie, who were rock-bottom of the old First Division at the time, came in mid-to-late January 1973. Did we let Billy go too soon? His Airdrie debut came at Broomfield in a league match against Celtic, then 25 points ahead of Airdrie at the other end of the league. Billy equalised for Airdrie, before Kevin McCann scored the winner in a famous 2-1 win for The Diamonds…

In July 1974 Billy, who was also employed as a fulltime joiner at Shawfield, left Airdrie and re-joined East Stirling as one of Alex, now Sir Alex, Ferguson's first signings for the club. It was rumoured that Billy cost him his entire transfer kitty of £2,000!

| | |
|---|---|
| **DATE** | Saturday 23rd September 1972 |
| **TOURNAMENT** | League Division Two |
| **FINAL SCORE** | Clyde 3 Albion Rovers 1 |
| **TEAM** | *Cairney, Anderson, Swan; Houston, Burns, Ahern; Sullivan, Beattie, Millar, McGrain and Boyle Sub Hulston* |
| **SCORER(S)** | *Swan, Millar, McGrain* |
| **ATTENDANCE** | 1402 |
| **REPORTER** | Jim Hutchison |

As Clyde approached this the sixth league match of the season, they sat in fourth position with their three wins and two draws providing eight points from five games, and we were still unbeaten in the league. Both Stirling Albion and Cowdenbeath were above us in the league, both having won all six of their matches thus far. So, even this early in the season, it was becoming imperative that Clyde win to keep in touch with the leaders.

*Alan Swan and Sam Millar go for the high ball, while Danny McGrain looks on..*

Albion Rovers had not played first division football since 1949 and were often referred to as a "Cinderella" club. They were managed by former Kilmarnock captain Frank Beattie, and as always led by the charismatic director Tom Fagan, who generally kept the club afloat by finding young talent and selling them on. Probably the most famous "name" of this era would be Scottish internationalist Tony Green, however goalkeeper Jim Brown, who played in this match against the Bully Wee, would also go on to be capped for Scotland whilst he was with Sheffield United.

In keeping with their traditions, they had, like Clyde that season, raided the junior ranks and unearthed a striking gem called Peter Dickson from Baillieston Juniors. Like our Peter Boyle, he too was enjoying life in his first senior season. Our defence would need to shackle him tightly.

Clyde started the match brightly enough and peppered the Rovers goal but found Jim Brown between the "sticks" in fine form, and it was mainly thanks to his performance that – astonishingly – the sides trooped off at half time all square, without a goal at either end.

They say that managers earn their money at half time and certainly Archie Robertson pulled a masterstroke at the interval in this match when he switched the full backs around, with Alan Swan moving to the right back berth and Eddie Anderson moving to the left back position.

The switch paid off almost immediately as Eddie Anderson's pass to Danny McGrain gave Danny the time to send a long ball forward into the path of the overlapping Swan, and he swept the ball past Brown to open the scoring, much to the relief and joy of the home support.

*Alan Swan and Sam Millar watch the ball head into the Rovers net…*

Sam Millar crashed home a second from a Dom Sullivan corner and Clyde were in "easy street" or so the fans thought. Clyde always want to make their fans sweat a bit and true to form that man Dickson struck in 68 minutes to bring Rovers back into the match, in a game where they had seldom threated. Danny McGrain restored order 9 minutes later, when he hit a spectacular third to finally clinch both points.

So, Clyde were still unbeaten and now faced two consecutive tough away matches that would test their championship credentials.

***Scoreflash…an equaliser for Danny…Willie McVie 1 Danny McGrain 1***

## The Ball-boy's Story...

Behind the goal at this match would probably have been ball-boy **Craig Rodger**. Craig's **dad John** wrote to the programme to tell them about Craig's unusual journey, and his dedication...

" Craig...went shopping with his mother and a friend on a recent Saturday on the promise that he would be free in time to do his duty for the "Bully Wee".

Alas, as 2:30 approached he was still far from the ground. A demonstration had meant bus chaos. So, my wife put him in a taxi, explaining to the driver that he was a ball-boy at Shawfield.

Give the driver his due, he flew across the city – right up to the Players' entrance at Shawfield. Out stepped Craig, all alone!

He is small for his age, and his appearance caused quite a bit of laughter at the main entrance when someone shouted

**"THINGS MUST BE GOOD WHEN EVEN THE BALL-BOYS ARRIVE BY TAXI!"**

## John Taylor: Then and Now (well almost!)

It isn't only players that we find featured in the "Official Match Day Programme" this season. In the issue for the home game against Albion Rovers a young **John Taylor** is featured with the then-editor of the programme Norman Brown. The headline reads "**Supporting Clyde is seven-days-a-week for John**".

John, of course, is still a very busy man throughout the week and on matchdays at Broadwood, and his involvement with the club has remained virtually unbroken, barring a short spell with Dundee United.

Currently John notes amongst his many other football involvements Vice-Chairman of Clyde FC and Editor of the award-winning Clyde View Match

Programme. His service with Clyde would have remained intact from the early seventies, had he not taken that wee sojourn to Dundee United (NB I'm assured there is no truth in the rumour that, in true Mattha Gemmell-style, he "*asked to get away every Setterday tae see the Clyde...*").

Anyway, the article focusses on John's passion for collecting Clyde programmes and newspaper cuttings, that had started back in the 60's, and introduced a new article to the programme to be written by John – "**GOLDEN CLYDE DAY'S OF THE 60's**".

John's hobby, nearly 50 years later, has helped make writing this book so much easier!

| DATE | Saturday 30th September 1972 |
|---|---|
| **TOURNAMENT** | League Division Two |
| **FINAL SCORE** | Berwick Rangers 0 Clyde 2 |
| **TEAM** | *Cairney, Anderson, Swan; Houston, Burns, Ahern; Sullivan,* |
| | *Beattie, Millar, McGrain and Thomson Sub Hulston* |
| **SCORER(S)** | *Beattie, Thomson* |
| **ATTENDANCE** | 531 |
| **REPORTER** | Gordon Sydney |

This was a potential "banana skin" for the Bully Wee if ever there was one - Berwick were still without a league win, and hadn't scored a home league goal thus far into the season!

And it was Berwick who very nearly opened the scoring in the first five minutes. An Ian Hall cross allowed Pat Wilson to put in a fine header that looked like a goal all the way until Phil Cairney leapt to make a fantastic fingertip save.

And that was just about that for Berwick. Clyde took complete control of the midfield after that, and could have racked up far more than just the two goals they scored.

It was Billy Beattie who opened the scoring in this game, twenty minutes after the kick-off, when he fairly hammered the ball past keeper Wilson. Ten minutes into the second half Colin Thomson eased the pressure when he took a pass in his stride, then beat two defenders before shooting past Wilson.

To perhaps illustrate the dominance Clyde had over a bottom-of-the-league Berwick, Billy Beattie had three further chances to complete his hat-trick that day. Two fine saves by keeper Wilson, and a further shot that beat Wilson but was cleared off the line by full-back Laing, all served to deny the Bully Wee a more comprehensive victory.

Still, the two points were most welcome.

| DATE | Saturday 7th October 1972 |
|---|---|
| TOURNAMENT | League Division Two |
| FINAL SCORE | Dunfermline Athletic 1 Clyde 2 |
| TEAM | *Cairney, Anderson, Swan; Houston, Burns, Ahern; Sullivan, McVie, Millar, McGrain and Boyle Sub McGoldrick* |
| SCORER(S) | *McVie, Sullivan* |
| ATTENDANCE | 4590 |
| REPORTER | Jim Hutchison |

Clyde headed to East End Park to face the Fifers in what would be their eighth league match of the season, only three of which had been at home. Our away form was certainly heartening though, and we were unbeaten; three victories and a draw down at Palmerston in the other match had brought seven points, and we were yet to concede a goal away from home in the league.

Dunfermline had been relegated along with Clyde the previous season, and like ourselves were equally determined to bounce straight back up to the First Division. Despite a shaky start to their campaign The Pars recent form was good, having drawn 0-0 with league leader Stirling Albion the previous week and prior to that having won three-in-a-row, netting 13 times in the process. It was clear their attacking style could cause a threat to our hitherto unbeaten record and "un-breached" defence (at least in away games)!

So, a stiff test awaited our lads and the match certainly lived up to the pre-match hype, as the first quarter of an hour witnessed Dunfermline attack pounding the Clyde defence. In the first ten minutes alone we conceded eight corners, with their big keeper John Arrol a virtual spectator. And, of course, here was another keeper who would take a turn between the sticks in later years for the Bully Wee, and with some distinction.

As so often happens in football the game turned on its head within a few minutes, with Clyde netting two quick goals. The first came in seventeen minutes from a distant free kick taken by Eddie Anderson. Big Willie McVie, playing at number eight, found himself unmarked and he gleefully nodded home. Three minutes later Dom Sullivan held off a desperate challenge by Jim Scott and crashed home a second.

Dom Sullivan must have enjoyed playing at East End Park; it was Dom who had scored our first goal in a thrilling 2-2 draw up there in our penultimate match of the previous season, to give us at least a fighting chance of avoiding relegation going into that fateful last match with Airdrie. Johnny Flanagan was our other scorer that day with Jim Leishman and a Barry Mitchell penalty counting for the Pars in what ultimately was an unsuccessful attempt to escape relegation for both clubs.

Meanwhile, those two goals took us through to the interval, with the half time discussion amongst the Clyde faithful largely focusing on whether (or not) a two-goal advantage would see the Bully Wee leaving with both points this time.

In the second period it was more of the same with Dunfermline laying siege in Clyde's half of the field, and they came very close to reducing the deficit when a certain Jim Leishman, playing at right back for the Pars that day, and trying no doubt to emulate Sullivan's achievement above, was just wide with a long range driven effort. Jim went on to be a wonderful servant to Dunfermline Athletic and his wit and good humour is legendary, but I am still glad he missed on this occasion!

Clyde's gallant defence held out until the 69th minute when Graham Shaw, easily Dunfermline's best player, headed in from a Dennis Nelson corner.

In an effort to shore up our clearly hard-pressed defence Archie Robertson took off Peter Boyle and brought on another centre half, in the shape of big Joe McGoldrick, with 14 minutes to go. This seemed to do the trick, but the match could have ended all square if Dennis Nelson had converted an absolutely golden chance in the last minute from a wonderful cross by Graham Shaw, a chance which he contrived to miss from barely a yard out!

| | P | W | D | L | Pts |
|---|---|---|---|---|---|
| Stirling A. | 10 | 8 | 2 | 0 | 18 |
| C'denbeath | 10 | 8 | 0 | 2 | 16 |
| Raith R. | 9 | 6 | 2 | 1 | 14 |
| St Mirren | 10 | 7 | 0 | 3 | 14 |
| **Clyde** | **8** | **6** | **2** | **0** | **14** |
| Dunfermline | 9 | 5 | 1 | 3 | 11 |
| Q.o.S. | 9 | 4 | 2 | 3 | 10 |
| Montrose | 9 | 5 | 0 | 4 | 10 |
| Hamilton | 10 | 4 | 1 | 5 | 9 |
| Forfar | 10 | 4 | 1 | 5 | 9 |
| Stenh's'muir | 7 | 3 | 1 | 3 | 7 |
| Clydebank | 10 | 3 | 1 | 6 | 7 |
| Albion R. | 9 | 3 | 1 | 5 | 7 |
| E. Stirling | 10 | 2 | 2 | 6 | 6 |
| Alloa A. | 7 | 2 | 1 | 4 | 5 |
| Queen's Pk. | 9 | 1 | 3 | 5 | 5 |
| Brechin C. | 10 | 2 | 1 | 7 | 5 |
| Berwick R. | 9 | 1 | 1 | 7 | 3 |
| Stranraer | 7 | 1 | 0 | 6 | 2 |

When the final whistle sounded, Clyde had maintained their unbeaten away record and had moved on to 14 points, level with St. Mirren and Raith Rovers in third place, two points behind Cowdenbeath, and only four points behind leaders Stirling Albion. We also had two games in hand to all the teams around us barring Raith Rovers, who would be our next opponents at Shawfield.

Every game seemed to be a four pointer at this stage and with the top of the league so tight there was no room for error.

***Scoreflash...Willie moves ahead...Willie McVie 2 Danny McGrain 1...***

**DATE**               Monday 9th October 1972
**TOURNAMENT**         Friendly
**FINAL SCORE**        Clyde 1 Scotland Pro-Youths 3
**SCORER(S)**          *Sullivan*
**REPORTER**           Gordon Sydney

Brian McLaughlin of Celtic was noted as a potential star of the future after his performance in this match. He set his side on the victory path with a glorious goal in the 30th minute. He burst through the middle on his own, weaved his way past three opponents then thundered a 15-yard volley into the net. After this Ken Mackie slammed home a perfect opening from Davie McNicoll in the 42nd minute for the young Scots. Within a minute Clyde scored when Sullivan converted a penalty, but with fourteen minutes to go McNicoll scored a third goal for the young Scots.

| | |
|---|---|
| **DATE** | Saturday 14<sup>th</sup> October 1972 |
| **TOURNAMENT** | League Division Two |
| **FINAL SCORE** | Clyde 3 Raith Rovers 0 |
| **TEAM** | *Cairney, Anderson, Swan; Houston, Burns, Ahern; Sullivan, McVie, Millar, McGrain and Boyle Sub Hulston* |
| **SCORER(S)** | *Sullivan, McVie, Boyle* |
| **ATTENDANCE** | 2175 |
| **REPORTER** | Graeme Clark |

Although a tad early to be billed a title decider, this was an important game in Clyde's emergence as genuine title contenders, coming as it did hard on the heels of the win over Dunfermline Athletic a week previous.

Going into the game, Raith sat in 3<sup>rd</sup> place, 4 points behind Leaders Stirling Albion, but level on points with The Bully Wee, who had a game in hand over their opponents.

Raith were managed by George Farm who had a tremendous track record, particularly with their Fife rivals Dunfermline who he guided to Scottish Cup glory in 1968 and, incredible as it seems now, to the semi-final of a major European Trophy – the old Cup Winners Cup – the following season. Now he managed a team who were one of the pre-season favourites for the title and included stars such as Joe Baker (ex-Torino, Man City & Hibs amongst others) and our very own former player Dick Staite, as well as a future Clyde player in Billy McLaren.

It was to be no happy return to Shawfield for Dick Staite's new team as Clyde turned in perhaps their best league performance of the season so far with a dazzling display of attacking football. In the first half in particular they tore the Raith defence to shreds, and it was no exaggeration to say they could have gone in at the break with more than three goals to show for their superiority.

Dom Sullivan rattled in the first in grand fashion in the 10<sup>th</sup> minute, running on to a free kick by Brian Ahern, before Willie McVie netted a right foot drive in the 21<sup>st</sup> minute, this time following a Sullivan free kick. This was the second goal of a "perfect hat-trick" for Willie. Against Dunfermline the previous week he had netted a header, and he would complete the feat the following week against Brechin City when he banged one in with his left. It was over three games but Willie surely deserves some leeway as a centre half, with more than a passing interest as an amateur boxer.

Clyde added a third on 31 minutes when Peter Boyle swept home a clever Sam Millar back heel to complete the scoring in a comprehensive victory over one of our main promotion rivals - the only disappointment being the lack of goals in the second half.

*Peter Boyle scores Clyde's third goal...*

Manager Archie Robertson was delighted, certainly with the win, but more so the performance...

*"**Excellent football – we really touched the type of game we have all been aiming for**"*

Smiles all round then for all connected with Shawfield. Although not for Dick Staite – as well as being on the wrong end of the scoreline, he also picked up a booking!

*Scoreflash...Willie moves further ahead...Willie McVie 3 Danny McGrain 1...*

## The Board of Directors / John Y Scoullar / John McBeth

The programme for this match opened with an obituary for Director John Scoullar, who passed away. John Young Scoullar was involved with Clyde for over sixty years, first as a player, then club secretary, and finally, from 1952 as a Director.

John was also a former referee, and was greatly respected in junior circles, and a member of the SFA Committee that introduced Under-23 internationals.

John's passing left a gap, thus in February 1973 John McBeth was appointed to the Board of Directors. John, of course, would go on to greater things in Scottish, European and World football.

This left the Clyde FC Board of Directors around this time as per the picture below...

(back row, l to r) G Johnstone, Dr J McCrorie, WJ (Billy) Dunn, JF McBeth
(front row, l to r) TL Clark, WP Dunn, IV Paterson

| | |
|---|---|
| **DATE** | Saturday 21st October 1972 |
| **TOURNAMENT** | League Division Two |
| **FINAL SCORE** | Brechin City 1 Clyde 3 |
| **TEAM** | *Cairney, Anderson, Swan; Houston, Burns, Ahern; Sullivan, McVie, Millar, McGrain and Boyle Sub Hulston* |
| **SCORER(S)** | *McVie, Boyle, Ahern* |
| **ATTENDANCE** | 481 |
| **REPORTER** | Alan Maxwell |

The Bully Wee started this one on the back of nine league games without defeat. Even more impressively, the two preceding games had brought maximum points against the teams many perceived to be favourites for promotion, the Fife pairing of Dunfermline Athletic and Raith Rovers. Given that Brechin were rock bottom of the table, it was fair to say that Clyde carried the favourites tag going into this match.

However, it was not "plain sailing"; Clyde being Clyde they lost the opener to a penalty kick. Alan Swan upended Brian Cooper in the 27th minute, the player dusted himself down before slamming the resultant penalty past a helpless Phil Cairney.

Seconds later Dom Sullivan had a chance to level, but smashed high over when well placed. Eddie Anderson followed suit just a few seconds later.

Clyde continued to press, so it was no great surprise when "the Boxer" Willie McVie was on hand to equalise when the home keeper could only parry a fierce shot from Captain courageous Danny McGrain (incidentally the third part of Willie's "treble"). Peter Boyle then received an unnecessary booking for some petulant retaliation.

The teams went in all square at the break, but classy Clyde were to shift up a few gears, and a packed home defence were struggling to cope with the pressure. Prompted in the main by Brian "Fishy" Ahern,

Clyde's total domination of the second half started just two minutes into it, when McVie turned into goal maker by supplying a clever cross for Peter Boyle to nod home.

In fifty-five minutes it was all over; Brian Ahern, easily Man-of-the-Match, was able to latch onto a misplaced throw out by Andy McEwan in the home goal, and net easily.

A lot of the credit went to gaffer Robertson for this well-planned away win. A proud manager told reporters...

*"We operated with a tightness at the back in anticipation of playing on a smaller pitch, but we modified our game as it went on, and it paid off"*

The new role created for former stopper Willie McVie was instrumental in gaining this victory. For the past three games stalwart Jimmy Burns had impressed in the centre-half role, with big Willie moving up front. Against Dunfermline Willie used his head, against Raith the previous Saturday he scored with his right foot and he bagged the equaliser in this one with his left peg – a unique hat-trick!

| | P | W | D | L | Pts |
|---|---|---|---|---|---|
| Stirling A. | 12 | 10 | 2 | 0 | 22 |
| **Clyde** | **10** | **8** | **2** | **0** | **18** |
| C'd'nbeath | 11 | 9 | 0 | 2 | 18 |
| St Mirren | 12 | 8 | 1 | 3 | 17 |
| Raith Rov. | 11 | 6 | 2 | 3 | 14 |
| D'nf'rmline | 10 | 6 | 1 | 3 | 13 |
| Hamilton | 12 | 6 | 1 | 5 | 13 |
| Q.o.S. | 11 | 5 | 2 | 4 | 12 |
| Montrose | 11 | 5 | 1 | 5 | 11 |
| Clydebank | 12 | 5 | 1 | 6 | 11 |
| Forfar | 12 | 4 | 2 | 6 | 10 |
| St'nh's'm'r | 10 | 3 | 2 | 5 | 8 |
| Alloa | 9 | 3 | 1 | 5 | 7 |
| E. Stirling | 12 | 2 | 3 | 8 | 7 |
| Albion R. | 11 | 3 | 1 | 7 | 7 |
| Queen's P. | 11 | 1 | 4 | 6 | 6 |
| Berwick | 11 | 2 | 2 | 7 | 6 |
| Stranraer | 10 | 2 | 1 | 7 | 5 |
| Brechin | 12 | 2 | 1 | 9 | 5 |

*Scoreflash...Willie moves even further ahead...Willie McVie 4 Danny McGrain 1*

| | |
|---|---|
| **DATE** | Saturday 28th October 1972 |
| **TOURNAMENT** | League Division Two |
| **FINAL SCORE** | Clyde 3 Stranraer 0 |
| **TEAM** | *Cairney, Anderson, Swan; Houston, Burns, Ahern; Sullivan, McVie, Millar, McGrain and Boyle Sub Hulston* |
| **SCORER(S)** | *Millar, Sullivan, McGrain* |
| **ATTENDANCE** | 1777 |
| **REPORTER** | Gordon Sydney |

Clyde wasted no time in getting into their stride.

Early on Dom Sullivan created the first chance of the match with a cross that Sam Millar headed for goal. Keeper Willie Whiteside could only parry the ball back into the path of Dom Sullivan, but Dom only managed to hit the side netting. A minute later Sam Millar also hit the side netting with a shot, then Stranraer's John Murray had plenty of time to pick his spot but he shot weakly past.

Whether this served a warning shot across the bows of the good ship Clyde or not, we took the lead in the 10th minute. Sam Millar wheeled sharply and hooked a fine shot past Whiteside. Willie McVie almost continued his fine scoring run, but his header came off the underside of the bar and was scrambled clear.

Stranraer held out until just two minutes after the break when man-of-the-match Dom Sullivan hit a tremendous 20-yarder into the net to double our advantage.

Our dominance continued into the second period, and the icing on the cake came with nine minutes left on the clock, and it should probably go down as a potential goal-of-the-season! Wee Danny McGrain, having a superb game, beat three defenders, played a one-two with Dom Sullivan, then simply sent his 25-yarder into the net. A beauty!

This result meant we had now won seven consecutive league games.

*Scoreflash...Danny pulls one back...Willie McVie 4 Danny McGrain 2...*

49

## Player Pic – Willie McVie                    Alan Maxwell

An interesting season for the hard man of the team. Willie had actually requested a transfer away from the club during the previous season. However, all was well for the start of the new season. In fact, the season couldn't have started any better for the big man. The opening game, a League Cup Sectional tie at home to Motherwell turned out an absolute corker. Inspired by the Billy McNeill's and Jackie Charlton's of the footballing world, Willie was encouraged by gaffer Robertson to visit the opposition penalty box for set piece moves, and Willie started the action by scoring our first competitive goal of the new season. He found his way into the 'Well box to head home a Brian Ahern corner. This was the first of half a dozen goals for the big man over the season.

Having been signed from junior outfit Lesmahagow in 1969, he was considered one of the more senior players at the ripe old age of 23! Given his ability to plug all the leaks in the Bully Wee defence, it was a bit of a coincidence that in civvy street he was a plumber to trade. Tall, good in the air and hard tackling on the deck, he had all the attributes of a competent centre-half. Nonetheless, he played a key role in Archie Robertson's mid-season masterstroke. Struggling for goals, and authority in the opposition penalty box, Willie was moved up into the front line, allowing Jimmy Burns to move seamlessly into centre-half, forming a fruitful partnership with Liam Houston. This was only possible thanks to the adaptability of the cultured McVie.

**Phil Cairney** provided an amusing anecdote about Willie…

*" We were up the East Coast somewhere, I can't remember where exactly – maybe Dunfermline or Kirkcaldy – and we always stopped off in Powfoulis for our pre-match lunch. Anyway, the bus sets off, and ten minutes or so into the journey I look out the bus window and there, sitting in a car alongside the bus, is Willie McVie! The bus had set off without checking we had a full complement of players!!! Needless to say, we stopped and picked big Willie up, so all was well in the end!!!"*

| | |
|---|---|
| **DATE** | Saturday 4th November 1972 |
| **TOURNAMENT** | League Division Two |
| **FINAL SCORE** | Hamilton Accies 2 Clyde 2 |
| **TEAM** | *Cairney, Anderson, Swan; Houston, Burns, Ahern; Sullivan, McVie, Millar, McGrain and Boyle Sub Hulston (for McVie)* |
| **SCORER(S)** | *Boyle (2)* |
| **ATTENDANCE** | 2835 |
| **REPORTER** | Jim Hutchison |

With Clyde having released so many players at the end of the previous season, it was almost inevitable that we would come up against some of them sooner or later.

A quick glance at the Hamilton Accies teamsheet quickly revealed that one of our legendary ex-players, Tommy McCulloch, would be their custodian that day. Tommy had long been a favourite of the Clyde supporters, and it certainly seemed strange to see him in goal at "the wrong end" of the pitch. Also lining up against us that day was our former midfield player Millar Hay (pictured), wearing the number 10 jersey.

Clyde were flying at this point in the season but Accies had been very unlucky the previous week, going down narrowly 2-1 to table-toppers Stirling Albion at Annfield, despite a great second half fightback.

So, on paper, this was no easy ride for Clyde at Douglas Park, with some former players looking to put one over their old club, and the local rivalry adding some "needle" to the proceedings – and so it proved.

Peter Boyle, our new outside left signed from the juniors only three months before, was being singled out for special praise in the press before the match, with Archie Robertson referring to him as Clyde's "Bobby Lennox" due to his knack of "*punishing goalkeepers mistakes and his "lightning reactions to the half chance*".

The praise of his manager must have had a positive effect on Peter for it was he who struck first for Clyde in 17 minutes, with a neat header from an Eddie

51

Anderson cross. This was the only strike of an excellent first half in front of a reported attendance of around 3000, but Clyde certainly were not having it all their own way in what was a thoroughly entertaining game for both sets of fans, with the game going from end-to-end.

*Football fans can be so fickle! For fifteen years we cheered every save Tommy McCulloch made. Now, we cheer when the ball goes past him and into the Hamilton net! Here, Peter Boyle has just put Clyde one up...*

Also playing for Accies that day, at centre-forward, was a certain Neil Hood who would later sign for Clyde and become – and remain - a real favourite of the Clyde fans who saw him play - and frequently score - in Clyde colours. It would, however, be fair to say that he wasn't the most popular player on the park in those parts of Douglas Park housing the Clyde support.

In the 49th minute, with three Clyde defenders backing off him, he took advantage of a clear look at goal and rifled the ball past Phil Cairney.

If that was a shock, then worse was to follow only ten minutes later when the same player chased down a poor passback by Alan Swan, collided with the on-rushing Cairney, and, as the ball broke loose, big Neilly prodded the ball into the empty net.

To say Danny McGrain was upset by the challenge on the keeper and the legality of the goal would be to put it mildly, and he carried his protest too far for the referee's liking, resulting in him being booked.

Our unbeaten record was hanging by a thread and as time ticked by it looked less and less likely to remain intact.

*Willie McVie challenges*
*Tommy McCulloch*

But, *"Cometh the Hour, Cometh the Man"*, and that man Boyle came to our rescue yet again. It was real tough luck on Tommy McCulloch who had done really well to block a shot from Liam Houston (although some reports said the initial shot was from Anderson). Either way Peter reacted quickest and followed up to nick a late equaliser in the 87th minute, salvaging a valuable point and keeping the unbeaten record going. Incidentally, these two goals took his tally to nine for the season, an astonishing return from the former Larkhall Thistle player.

Although Clyde certainly left it late to maintain their record at Douglas Park, their consistency was beginning to be noticed and reported in the National press. Clyde & Burnley were the only two unbeaten sides in British senior football by this stage of the season, with Clyde having the best goals against tally, only conceding a miserly eight in twelve league matches.

Although no one could know it at the time not only did Neil Hood go on to join Clyde from the line-up that day, but Gordon Hamilton also went on to sign for Clyde, in a double-signing by Stan Anderson a few years later.

Another youngster playing at number 8 that day did not too badly in his career either; a certain young Paul Hegarty, who went on to play in many fine Dundee United teams and gain international recognition.

Manager Archie Robertson expressed his satisfaction with the side's shooting ability...

*" One feature that has pleased me has been the way the players have been striking the ball – cleanly, compactly and frequently."*

*Peter Boyle hits a late equaliser against Hamilton Accies to maintain our unbeaten league record...*

This draw left the league table looking like this...

| | P | W | D | L | Pts |
|---|---|---|---|---|---|
| Stirling A. | 14 | 11 | 2 | 1 | 24 |
| **Clyde** | **12** | **9** | **3** | **0** | **21** |
| C'd'nbeath | 13 | 9 | 1 | 3 | 19 |
| St Mirren | 14 | 9 | 1 | 4 | 19 |
| D'nfrmline | 12 | 8 | 1 | 3 | 17 |
| Raith R. | 12 | 7 | 2 | 3 | 16 |
| Q.o.S. | 13 | 7 | 2 | 4 | 16 |
| Montrose | 13 | 6 | 2 | 5 | 14 |
| Hamilton | 14 | 6 | 2 | 6 | 14 |
| Forfar | 13 | 4 | 3 | 6 | 11 |
| Clydebank | 14 | 5 | 1 | 8 | 11 |
| St'nh's'm'r | 12 | 4 | 2 | 6 | 10 |
| Berwick | 13 | 4 | 2 | 7 | 10 |
| Alloa | 11 | 4 | 1 | 6 | 9 |
| E. Stirling | 14 | 3 | 3 | 8 | 9 |
| Albion R. | 13 | 4 | 1 | 8 | 9 |
| Queen's P. | 13 | 1 | 5 | 7 | 7 |
| Stranraer | 12 | 2 | 1 | 9 | 5 |
| Brechin | 14 | 2 | 1 | 11 | 5 |

| | |
|---|---|
| **DATE** | Saturday 11<sup>th</sup> November 1972 |
| **TOURNAMENT** | League Division Two |
| **FINAL SCORE** | Clyde 1 Stenhousemuir 3 |
| **TEAM** | *Cairney, Anderson, Swan; Houston, Burns, Ahern; Sullivan,* |
| | *McVie, Millar, McGrain and Boyle Sub Hulston* |
| **SCORER(S)** | *McVie* |
| **ATTENDANCE** | 1537 |
| **REPORTER** | Gordon Sydney |

It might have been Armistice Day 1972, but there was a battle to be fought at Shawfield Stadium that day; in the white shirts, we had the Bully Wee, second top of the league and protecting the last unbeaten league record in Scotland twelve matches into the season; whilst in the maroon shirts there were The Warriors from Ochilview, sitting mid-table.

If we needed any warning, it came a week previous. Whilst Clyde were drawing at Douglas Park, Stenhousemuir were putting an end to Stirling Albion's unbeaten league run. Also worth noting was that although it had been nine seasons since Stenhousemuir had visited Shawfield Stadium, it wouldn't be a new experience for at least one of the Stenhousemuir players – former Clyde defender and captain Harry Glasgow (pictured) was playing at centre-forward for The Warriors.

It only took Stenhousemuir five minutes to move into the lead, a Martin Boyle cut-back being fired past Phil Cairney by Andy Scobie. If that was a shock to the system, even worse was to follow just two minutes later when Jim Burns handled a through ball, and from the penalty spot Jim Wight gave Phil Cairney his second opportunity to gather the ball from the back of the net.

The remainder of the first half – and virtually the entire remainder of the match – was played out in the Stenhousemuir half, with the away side looking to hit on the break. Just a minute before half time a chink of light appeared at the end of a long tunnel, when Willie McVie, another player playing in an unaccustomed role as centre-forward, put one past future Scotland keeper Stewart Kennedy.

So, the battle was well and truly on for the second half; the siege of Shawfield was about to start. However, it didn't go according to plan, and nine minutes from the end a through ball from Harry Glasgow found Alan Hughes, and he scored Stenhousemuir's third goal, the final goal of the game.

So, Clyde's unbeaten league record was undone, but the Bully Wee weren't the only unbeaten team in British senior football that day; English Division Two (now the Championship) side Burnley were in a similar position, although they had played 16 league matches. They were at home to Leyton Orient, but in a strange parallel with the Bully Wee they were also beaten at home, so the two longest unbeaten league records in Britain went on the same day.

*Scoreflash...Big Willie goes nap...Willie McVie 5 Danny McGrain 2...*

| | |
|---|---|
| **DATE** | Saturday 18<sup>th</sup> November 1972 |
| **TOURNAMENT** | League Division Two |
| **FINAL SCORE** | East Stirling 0 Clyde 5 |
| **TEAM** | *Cairney, Anderson, Swan; Houston, Burns, Ahern; Sullivan, McGuinness, Millar, McGrain and Boyle Sub Hulston (for Millar)* |
| **SCORER(S)** | *Own Goal, Boyle (2), Sullivan, Hulston* |
| **ATTENDANCE** | 754 |
| **REPORTER** | Gordon Sydney |

So how would the team react to their first league defeat?

On the eve of the match, with snow forecast, Manager Archie Robertson wasn't taking any chances – "*I'll wait until I see ground conditions before naming a side*". In the end the only team change Archie made was to bring in Eddie McGuinness to replace Willie McVie. Substitute Billy Hulston retained his place on the bench, so big Willie, despite his goal last Saturday, was out altogether!

When the match got underway, "both sides found the conditions underfoot very tricky", but we still managed at least a couple of close things in the first half. Peter Boyle had a shot from 18-yards, and Eddie McGuinness had a fine header on goal, both of which were saved by keeper Bert Archibald.

The second half was a different story, and it all started less than a minute after the restart. Peter Boyle got down the right wing, swung his cross over, and defender Simpson put through his own goal whilst trying to clear. The 'Shire came back at us, and had a couple of shots, but our lead was cemented in 74 minutes when Billy Hulston, by this time on as sub for Sam Millar, crossed for Peter Boyle to score. After this the home defence caved in, and there followed an avalanche of goals.

Two minutes later Dom Sullivan made it three with a goal described as "one of the best ever seen at Firs Park" when he rifled in a 25-yard free-kick, then a mere three minutes later, in the 79<sup>th</sup> minute, Peter Boyle got Clyde's fourth.

Three goals in five minutes was excellent, however we weren't finished, and in the 83<sup>rd</sup> minute we made it four goals in nine minutes when former East Stirling striker Billy Hulston pushed the ball home after a goalmouth scramble to round off an excellent day at the "office"!

The East Stirling programme that day started with the words "Our visitors today Clyde FC are having a good season...", and at the end of this ninety minutes it was right back to being a good season! The team could hardly have given a more positive response to the cautious question posed right at the start of this report. Five goals, a clean sheet and of course two points put us right back on track, Stirling Albion had their Saturday off, so not only did we close the gap on the league leaders, but we gave ourselves the opportunity to go top with a win at Shawfield next Saturday, when of course the visitors just had to be Stirling Albion!

Stewarding at football matches is still the cause of much consternation at football matches these days, and seems it was an issue even back in the early-seventies, as *Jim Hutchison* remembers..." when *Billy Hulston ran riot at Firs Park against East Stirling, me and my then youthful pals had somehow gone into the Grandstand. Now by even those years standards the "Grandstand" at Firs Park was laughable, and by today's standards it certainly wouldn't get a safety certificate. Anyway, as the goals went in, we would stamp our feet, and eventually we were ejected by some wee officious man for making too much noise! Too much noise at a football game! You cannae make it up!!!"*

*That pesky Firs Park Stand...*

## Dom Sullivan capped

Monday 20<sup>th</sup> November will go down as the day Dom Sullivan pulled on his first Scotland Under-23 jersey. It was of course a significant honour for the club as well, but served to illustrate the skills and abilities of Dom, considering he was playing for a Second Division team at the time.

Dom, typically, played it down…" *It was a great feeling pulling that Scotland jersey over my head, but I don't feel individually any better than the rest of my team-mates, for I was really the representative chosen to carry the flag for the club, as it were. This was the outcome of a team effort. I don't for a minute think it will be the last time one of the present Clyde team will pull on a Scotland jersey."*

Dom also remarked that "*on a cold dismal night at Easter Road it was a great lift, especially in the early stages, to hear the shouts of Clyde supporters who had travelled through to Edinburgh for the game*", and he also thanked "*our manager and all my team-mates for the help they gave me on this occasion*."

Dom was "*reasonably happy with my first half display, but I tired a bit in the second half*."

The newspapers, though, were mightily impressed…

- The Glasgow Herald considered "*Sullivan [was] one of the best players on view*"
- The Evening Times wrote "*Another youngster who caught the eye was Clyde's Dom Sullivan…he was one of the big successes of the evening*"
- The Scotsman noted "*The last Clyde player to wear the navy blue of Scotland was Harry Hood, now of Celtic. That was in 1968. When will the next be? Not too distant on present form*"

| | |
|---|---|
| **DATE** | Saturday 25<sup>th</sup> November 1972 |
| **TOURNAMENT** | League Division Two |
| **FINAL SCORE** | Clyde 1 Stirling Albion 1 |
| **TEAM** | *Cairney, Anderson, Swan; Burns, Houston, Ahern; Sullivan, McGuinness, Millar, McGrain and Boyle Sub Hulston (for McGuinness)* |
| **SCORER(S)** | *Boyle* |
| **ATTENDANCE** | 2667 |
| **REPORTER** | Gordon Sydney |

The Clash of the Titans!

The long-awaited top-of-the-table clash between the two early pacesetters got underway, and we didn't have to wait long for the action to start.

A fine passing move between Danny McGrain and Dom Sullivan allowed Peter Boyle to fire off a screamer that keeper Young saved at full stretch, but that only delayed our opening goal.

With only five minutes on the clock, Eddie Anderson, overlapping, sent in a cross that Danny McGrain slipped through to Peter Boyle. Peter, in the clear, sent it past keeper Young.

One nil, the perfect start (unless you were reading the programme and mostly missed it)!

Clyde had been so much on the front foot that virtually Phil Cairney's first touch was to deal with a Jim Burns passback, and still we maintained the pressure. Dom Sullivan's cross was headed out by Bill McGarry, then a combination of good work between Danny McGrain and Eddie McGuinness brought a corner, which was again cleared by McGarry.

Stirling then ventured upfield, and a corner was headed narrowly past by McPhee, before "normal service" was resumed. Sam Millar brought out an excellent save from Young, then Dom Sullivan's trickery forced not one but two corners in quick succession, and from the second Sam Millar headed narrowly wide.

Stirling showed another glimpse of their capabilities when McGarry swung a long ball out to Steele, and his cross forced Alan Swan into conceding a corner, which ultimately came to nothing.

And still Clyde pressed. Busy Stirling keeper Young only just managed to divert Dom Sullivan's cross away from Sam Millar's head, but in another breakaway Steele couldn't get enough power in his header from McPhee's cross to trouble Phil Cairney.

Would we live to regret all this pressure with only a goal to show for it? Yes, because in the dying minutes, with the referee looking at his watch, up at the Tote end, Gus McMillan snatched an equaliser for Stirling Albion to stun the Bully Wee faithful.

Stirling Albion, to their credit, had weathered the storm and had come right back into the game in the second half. Helped no doubt by the appearance as a 63rd minute substitute of former Clyde player Andy Stevenson, still a loyal Clyde supporter to this day!

*Peter Boyle challenges Stirling Albion keeper George Young, with Billy Hulston and Sam Millar looking on.*

| | |
|---|---|
| **DATE** | Saturday 2nd December 1972 |
| **TOURNAMENT** | League Division Two |
| **FINAL SCORE** | Clyde 2 Cowdenbeath 1 |
| **TEAM** | *Cairney, Anderson, Swan; Burns, Houston, Ahern; Sullivan, McGuinness, Millar, McGrain and Boyle Sub Hulston (for McGuinness)* |
| **SCORER(S)** | *Ahern, Millar* |
| **ATTENDANCE** | 1648 |
| **REPORTER** | Graeme Clark |

Clyde went into this match two points ahead of their opponents, and two points behind league leaders Stirling Albion, but with a game in hand to both teams, so victory was important to not only maintain a challenge to the leaders but also to create a bit of space between the leaders and the challenging pack. And yet again a former Clyde favourite lined up in opposition colours, this time it was Alex Bryce, pictured.

Cowdenbeath, however, had not read the script, and shocked the home team with a goal after just two minutes when defender Jim Taylor headed a corner past Cairney. Perhaps this early goal persuaded Cowdenbeath to "park the bus", or maybe that had been their intention all along but either way the Fifers retreated into a defensive shell which Clyde found difficult to pierce – partly due to doughty defending but mainly because of a succession of missed opportunities.

Clyde pushed forward after the early setback with Alan Swan having the best effort of the early pressure when he unleashed a vicious drive from 25 yards that Cowden keeper Ray Alan did well to turn over the bar. Eventually, though, the pressure told and Clyde grabbed a deserved equaliser. Ray Allan could only punch away an indirect free kick in the box. In the stramash that followed, Eddie McGuinness's net bound shot was palmed onto the bar by Alan Reid, one of 10 Cowden players in the six-yard box. Penalty! A little bit of history was made here as Brian Ahern stepped up to take his first penalty kick for the Club and, of course, to score - the start of a long and successful penalty-taking career!

With Captain Danny McGrain pulling the strings with his passing and clever touches, Clyde created numerous more chances before the break with Sullivan, Ahern, Millar and McGrain himself all missing chances. Ahern, in particular, should have done better with the goal at his mercy but he delayed his shot allowing the Fife defence to clear.

The second half was a similar tale of Clyde pressing forward and passing up chances against a Cowdenbeath side determined to prevent a second goal and perhaps grab one of their own on the break. Indeed, Phil Cairney had to produce a tremendous save at point blank range to deny the Fifers. Midway through the second half, Manager Robertson decided that enough was enough and took off McGuinness (not a wholly popular decision with the Clyde support) and brought on Billy Hulston. Eventually the goal that proved to be the winner arrived, with Sam Millar netting on 77 minutes. Dom Sullivan swung over a corner and Sam was in the right place to head home.

Just as Cowdenbeath's early goal had perhaps influenced them to sit back, so Millar's goal had the opposite effect and for the last 10 minutes it was Clyde's turn to be pinned back. But the team held out to pick up another two points in the quest for the Championship, although if the fans were looking for something to worry about it was our seeming inability to turn outfield superiority into a more comprehensive victory.

Around this time manager **Archie Robertson** gave a wee interview to the Evening Times about Tommy Docherty's task of moulding Scotland into a team capable of winning the 1974 World Cup! Although Archie's answer is based on that hypothetical event, I'm sure it can be aligned with his approach at the Bully Wee…

*"It's a case of building a team. For this you don't necessarily need a team of great players. The basic of building a team is to have a variety. You need runners, ball players, hard men. You need a blend."*

## Player Pic – Brian Ahern                    Graeme Clark

Season 1972/73 saw the emergence of a man who would in time become Captain of Clyde and a real stalwart during the seventies and eighties, in two separate spells with the Club. Brian Ahern would end his time with Clyde in 1987 as our leading player in terms of league appearances (424) and his outstanding service to the Bully Wee would see him deservedly inducted into the Clyde FC Hall of Fame.

All this, however, lay ahead of Brian.

Season 71/72 had been a mixed bag for him, in and out of the team, and not really establishing himself as a first team regular; hardly surprising given his tender years and the poor form of the team in general. Season 1972/73 changed all that, thanks to Clyde's policy of giving youth its chance. Aged just 20 at the start of the season, Brian went on to make 41 appearances in all, chipping in with 10 goals, including 5 penalties, a fine return from a man who played most of the season on the left side of midfield.

Ahern was a truly talented footballer, tenacious in the tackle, skilful and blessed with a sweet left foot. His intelligent use of the ball was a delight to behold and he had a tremendous enthusiasm for the game, and it was in this season he started to acquire a reputation as a dead ball expert. Free kicks, corners and most effectively – penalties. Over his years with Clyde he would take 41 spot kicks, converting the vast majority of them, with his first ever penalty being tucked away in the 2-1 home league win over Cowdenbeath in December of this season.

Brian Ahern once said that his favourite player was the renowned German midfielder of the day, Gunther Netzer, a man who was, according to Ahern, "......so deadly accurate with his passing.........a treat to watch". It's a description that Clyde fans would happily use to describe Brian this season, and indeed for many other seasons thereafter.

| DATE | Saturday 9th December 1972 |
|---|---|
| **TOURNAMENT** | League Division Two |
| **FINAL SCORE** | Alloa Athletic 0 Clyde 0 |
| **TEAM** | *Cairney, Anderson, Swan; Burns, Houston, Ahern; Sullivan, Hulston, Millar, McGrain and Boyle Sub McGuinness (for Ahern)* |
| **ATTENDANCE** | 927 |
| **REPORTER** | Gordon Sydney |

Being only two points behind Stirling Albion, with a game in hand, meant we really wanted the victory to move level with them and make a statement as to our intentions. Although in the end only a single point was achieved, it wasn't for the want of trying, especially in the first half.

As frequently happened this season, Dave McWilliams, the Alloa keeper on the day, would go on to keep goal for the Bully Wee in the late seventies and early eighties.

Clyde came out with all guns blazing, and moved the ball around with accuracy and purpose. Dom Sullivan was having a fine game on the wing, and Sam Millar had a couple of good shots on goal in the first ten minutes. Then Peter Boyle, from six yards, could only put the ball into home keeper Dave McWilliams hands. McWilliams then pulled off a good save to deny Danny McGrain, but when the keeper was finally beaten, Peter Boyle's header came back off the bar.

The second half wasn't so impressive for Clyde. Seemingly losing their poise, the most noteworthy moment came when Liam Houston was caught out at the back. Joe McCallan got the ball off him, and fired in a shot that beat Phil Cairney but came back to safety off the inside of the post.

So, was this a point gained or a point lost? The guy who cracked the ball off of the inside of the post in the second half, Joe McCallan, had hit two the previous Saturday when the Wasps beat Hamilton Accies 3-0 away at Douglas Park. All Alloa's goals came in a second half blitz and that meant they were unbeaten in their previous 5 games before facing Clyde, so maybe it wasn't so bad a result on reflection.

Meanwhile, on the terracing, Clyde fans unfamiliar with Second Division grounds could easily get lost, or a bit mixed up. **David Cunningham** tells us this story about such an incident...

*"Season 72/73 in the Second Division gave me my first opportunity to visit some of the smaller grounds with my father. A rushed arrival at Recreation Park, Alloa, just before kick-off was a memorable occasion. We transferred to the old "Orange Box" Stand and took a couple of turns along a corridor. I turned to see my father about to take a seat beside manager Archie Robertson on a wooden bench which constituted the dugout. A hasty retreat with red faces akin to the Clyde away strip ensued!"*

*The Old Stand at Recreation Park Alloa*

| | |
|---|---|
| **DATE** | Saturday 16th December 1972 |
| **TOURNAMENT** | Friendly |
| **FINAL SCORE** | Clyde 6 Brora Rangers 0 |
| **REPORTER** | Gordon Sydney |

With Clyde's scheduled visitors Clydebank still involved in the Scottish Cup, Clyde were left facing a blank Saturday. Brora Rangers also had a blank Saturday, but it seems they may have been playing Clyde with an ulterior motive in mind (other than to have a weekend away in Glasgow just before Christmas!), given they were due to face Clyde's Division Two rivals Hamilton Accies in a Scottish Cup match. Of course, it also gave Accies representatives the chance to watch their Cup opponents close at hand!

In the end, it probably served Clyde better, with six goals to show without reply against the Highland league outfit. Peter Boyle got his first senior hat-trick, albeit not in a competitive match, scoring three of our five goals in the first half.

*Shawfield Stadium*

A single goal in the second half brought an end to the goalscoring.

Footnote: The Brora Rangers v Hamilton Accies Scottish Cup match up at Dudgeon Park ended in a 4-0 win for the Accies, so perhaps the opportunity didn't quite benefit the Highlanders as much as they envisaged!

| DATE | Saturday 23rd December 1972 |
|---|---|
| TOURNAMENT | League Division Two |
| FINAL SCORE | St Mirren 0 Clyde 1 |
| TEAM | *Cairney, Anderson, Swan; Burns, Houston, Ahern; Sullivan, McVie, Millar, McGrain and Boyle Sub McHugh (for Ahern)* |
| SCORER(S) | *Sullivan* |
| ATTENDANCE | 4193 |
| REPORTER | Jim Hutchison |

There was much excitement building up among the supporters of both sides before this game, the last match of the year at Love Street, and a bumper crowd of 4193 rolled up to take in the action.

Both sides had been idle as far as league matches were concerned the previous week, but prior to that The Saints had been in fine form, having swept Hamilton Accies off the Park 7-1 in their previous home game. That match was a personal triumph for the big Saints centre forward Gus McLeod, who helped himself to FIVE of those seven goals! Joe Harper had moved from Aberdeen to Everton, so Gus was right at the top of the scoring charts, along with Jim O'Rourke of Hibs, Dundee's John Duncan and another Second Division striker, Joe Baker of Raith Rovers, all of whom were on 22 goals for the season.

Clyde, though, would certainly be a much tougher nut to crack than Hamilton Accies, and had themselves hit Brora Rangers for six in a hastily-arranged friendly the week before.

Good news for Clyde fans before the match was that our longest serving player John McHugh was recalled to the squad for the first time that season. John was listed on the substitutes bench in place of young Eddie McGuinness, which suggested that Clyde were going to play it tight.

In truth the first half owed little to graceful football on a bitter cold day, and was a hard, punishing, game filled with bad feeling and numerous niggling fouls. The referee was Mr J.C. McRoberts of Wishaw, and he was the busiest man afield as he booked McGrain, McVie and Burns of Clyde and Munro of St. Mirren.

After an indifferent start Clyde began to take control, mainly through the efforts of club captain Danny McGrain, who was being compared in many

68

quarters of the press to Billy Bremner due to his style of play and endless enthusiasm.

Deadlocked it was until Clyde took the lead in the 37th minute - and what a corker it was!

After some fine leading up play by that seemingly perpetual motion man Danny McGrain, he passed to Dom Sullivan, who hammered in a stunning 20-yard strike which, although Danny Stevenson, the Paisley keeper, got his hands to, he couldn't keep it out.

In the second half Clyde played some great one touch football and the Saints in truth faded out of the game. John McHugh had come off the bench to replace Brian Ahern, and was desperately unlucky not to make a dream return, after a great strike came rattling back into play off the crossbar.

At the final whistle even better news greeted the Clyde faithful through their transistor radios - no Sky or internet in the 70's - in the shape of the result from Hampden that Queens Park had beaten league leaders Stirling Albion. This meant Clyde were now only one point behind the league leaders in second place but significantly with a game in hand.

| | P | W | D | L | Pts |
|---|---|---|---|---|---|
| Stirling A. | 19 | 13 | 4 | 2 | 30 |
| **Clyde** | **18** | **12** | **5** | **1** | **29** |
| Raith Rov | 20 | 10 | 5 | 4 | 27 |
| C'd'nbeath | 20 | 12 | 3 | 5 | 27 |
| D'nf'rmline | 19 | 12 | 2 | 5 | 26 |
| St Mirren | 19 | 11 | 2 | 6 | 24 |
| Montrose | 19 | 9 | 4 | 6 | 22 |
| Q.o.S. | 20 | 9 | 4 | 7 | 22 |
| St'nh's'm'r | 18 | 9 | 2 | 7 | 20 |
| Berwick R. | 19 | 8 | 3 | 8 | 19 |
| Hamilton | 20 | 7 | 3 | 10 | 17 |
| Alloa Ath. | 18 | 5 | 6 | 7 | 16 |
| Queen's P. | 20 | 4 | 7 | 9 | 15 |
| Forfar Ath. | 20 | 4 | 5 | 10 | 14 |
| Stranraer | 19 | 6 | 1 | 12 | 13 |
| Clydebank | 18 | 5 | 1 | 12 | 11 |
| Albion R. | 19 | 4 | 3 | 11 | 11 |
| E. Stirling | 19 | 3 | 4 | 12 | 10 |
| Brechin C. | 18 | 4 | 1 | 13 | 9 |

So, we all were off to enjoy a very Merry Christmas and Clyde were looking good to take over top spot in the New Year.

## Lies, Damn Lies and Statistics

This victory over St Mirren might represent a wee bit of club history, in that it could be our 1000th league victory! At the start of season 1939/40, we won one game out of the five played. That league was cancelled, and football re-organised for the duration of the war. So, if you ignore that victory, but include all (other) wartime fixtures, then this was our 1000th league victory.

As I said, lies, damn lies and statistics...

# Player Pic – Dom Sullivan

**Graeme Clark and Alan Maxwell**

Signed from junior club St Roch's in 1969, Dom Sullivan was recognised as an outstanding attacking talent, equally at home playing through the middle or on the right wing. Dom immediately impressed consistently with the Bully Wee second string, and duly made his first team debut at Love Street in an impressive 1-0 win against St. Mirren. With manager Archie Robertson rebuilding the side, Dom was to form an integral part of the famous "Robertson babes", and he remained a regular first-teamer for the six seasons he was at Shawfield.

During season 72/73, manager Robertson astutely switched the promising youngster to a more creative midfield role where he was able, with great effect, to influence the play around him.

Sullivan enjoyed a fantastic promotion season with Clyde, his crosses (delivered with either foot) were a fearsome weapon, and he was also a recognised scorer of chances, not just a creator. Indeed, he found the back of the net from midfield on 11 occasions, from 36 starts.

The player was rewarded for his fine form with a Scotland call up, taking the field for the Under 23-side under the floodlights of Easter Road, the first Clyde player since Harry Hood in 1968 to gain representative honours. As Sullivan was quick to acknowledge, the honour was a reflection of the efforts of his team-mates as much as his own form. He had an outstanding game, fully justifying his selection, as the Glasgow Herald noted "Sullivan...was one of the best players on view". Dom went on to further Under-23 honours in future seasons.

Dom was subject to intense transfer speculation throughout the season, with rumours including that the mighty Leeds United team of that time were interested, but Clyde's valuation of the player deterred them. However, in 1976 he moved to Aberdeen, winning the League Cup that same year, before joining Celtic in 1979 where further honours followed including consecutive league titles.

| | |
|---|---|
| **DATE** | Saturday 30<sup>th</sup> December 1972 |
| **TOURNAMENT** | League Division Two |
| **FINAL SCORE** | Clyde 2 Montrose 2 |
| **TEAM** | *Cairney, Anderson, Swan; Burns, Houston, Ahern; Sullivan, McVie, Millar, McGrain and Boyle Sub McHugh* |
| **SCORER(S)** | *Millar, Ahern (pen)* |
| **ATTENDANCE** | 1768 |
| **REPORTER** | Gordon Sydney |

The penultimate day of a tumultuous year brought Montrose to Shawfield in a match that was to be a prelude to our forthcoming Scottish Cup tie against the Gable Endies.

Clyde, attacking the Tote end at Shawfield, were first out the blocks, and Denis D'Arcy had to clear smartly from Peter Boyle. The action went up the other end, with Montrose centre forward Brian Third's shot striking the post and bouncing clear. Willie McVie, again playing a more attacking role, was causing problems in the away defence, but in the 21<sup>st</sup> minute it was that man Brian Third that opened the scoring. One-on-one with Phil Cairney following a through ball that Liam Houston just failed to intercept, his first shot was against Phil Cairney's body, but he successfully netted the rebound.

*Sam Millar*

Both keepers were being kept warm on this cold December day; first, not long after the opening goal, Gordon Crammond's cross-shot brought out a good save from Phil Cairney; then, a few minutes later, a good Willie McVie header had Phil's opposite number George Whisker looking smart to save. The last action of the first half saw Phil neatly saving a crisp shot from Bobby Livingston.

Seventeen minutes into the second half and Clyde were left a mountain to climb when Bobby Livingston rounded Liam Houston and fairly bulged the net behind Phil Cairney to double Montrose's lead. A few minutes later Brian Third again hit the post for the second time in the match, but matters thereafter seemed to pick up for the Bully Wee, and in the 75th minute Sam Millar halved the deficit with a diving header.

The late drama was reserved for the Montrose penalty area, and just before the final whistle Montrose full-back Peter Urquhart was adjudged by referee Callaghan to have handled the ball. Brian Ahern stepped up, took the pressure and the ball in his stride, and equalised.

Speaking to Brian recently, he was honest enough to admit this hadn't been one of his better games, as he was carrying an injury, and he expected to have to "walk the plank" past disgruntled supporters. Instead his equalising penalty in the final minute capped a great fightback, brought an unexpected point, so all was as well as it could have been given the situation just fifteen minutes or so beforehand.

With Stirling Albion not playing, this point brought us level with the Bino's both on points and games played, although we remained second in the league on Goal Difference.

| | |
|---|---|
| **DATE** | Monday 1$^{st}$ January 1973 |
| **TOURNAMENT** | League Division Two |
| **FINAL SCORE** | Queens Park 1 Clyde 3 |
| **TEAM** | *Cairney, Anderson, Swan; Burns, McGoldrick, McHugh; Harvey, Houston, Millar, McGrain and Boyle Sub McGuinness* |
| **SCORER(S)** | *Harvey, Boyle (2)* |
| **ATTENDANCE** | 2004 |
| **REPORTER** | Gordon Sydney |

So, this was it!

A New Year, and a new ground for me - my first-ever visit to Hampden.

Making the news for the Bully Wee was a guy not much older than me, Bobby Harvey. Seventeen years old, still at school, was making his debut at the old stadium, in place of the injured Dom Sullivan. And what a debut he had...

Fifteen minutes into the match the ball reaches young Bobby out on the stand side wing, not very far away from us in the enclosure. So, what does Bobby do? Only hits a cracking shot right into the back of the net...What a start!

There was the ubiquitous blip midway through the first half, when Joe McGoldrick was adjudged to have fouled Ally Scott in the box and Malky MacKay stepped up to equalise.

Peter Boyle, without a goal in his last four matches, was back, and his shot on the 28$^{th}$ minute mark – again a first-timer from outside the box – fairly flew into the net to give the Bully Wee a nice lead at half time.

The second half saw, predictably, Queens Park come out and give it a right go. However, twelve minutes into the half Liam Houston and Peter Boyle contrived to pass their way through the home defence, leaving Peter facing goalkeeper Taylor. Peter coolly rounded the keeper, and sent the ball into the empty net to put us in pole position, a position that we held until the final whistle.

This was just one of those days when everything in the world goes according to plan; I get my trip to see Hampden; Bobby Harvey scores a cracker on his debut; and of course, the Bully Wee earn themselves two more league points.

Bobby recalled the match a couple of years ago when I spoke with him...

*" I remember getting the phone call from Archie Robertson to bring my boots over to Hampden Park, but I never really thought too much about it, but turned out Danny [McGrain] and Dom [Sullivan] were injured and I was playing. One thing I remember about the game was the sheer size of the pitch – I was taking corners but couldn't get my crosses into the centre of the box"*

Most importantly though, with Stirling Albion losing at Love Street, Clyde were top of the league for the first time this season. 1973 looked like it would be a good year....

| | P | W | D | L | Pts |
|---|---|---|---|---|---|
| **Clyde** | **20** | **13** | **6** | **1** | **32** |
| Stirling A. | 20 | 13 | 4 | 3 | 30 |
| C'denbeath | 22 | 13 | 3 | 6 | 29 |
| D'nf'rmlin' | 21 | 13 | 2 | 6 | 28 |
| St Mirren | 21 | 12 | 3 | 6 | 27 |
| Raith R. | 21 | 11 | 5 | 5 | 27 |
| Montrose | 21 | 10 | 5 | 6 | 25 |
| Q.o.S. | 22 | 9 | 5 | 8 | 23 |
| Berwick R. | 20 | 9 | 3 | 8 | 21 |
| St'nh's'm'r | 19 | 9 | 2 | 8 | 20 |
| Hamilton | 22 | 8 | 4 | 10 | 20 |
| Alloa Ath. | 20 | 6 | 6 | 8 | 18 |
| Stranraer | 21 | 7 | 2 | 12 | 16 |
| Forfar Ath. | 22 | 5 | 6 | 11 | 16 |
| Queen's P. | 22 | 4 | 7 | 11 | 15 |
| E. Stirling | 21 | 4 | 5 | 12 | 13 |
| Clydebank | 19 | 5 | 2 | 12 | 12 |
| Albion R. | 20 | 4 | 4 | 12 | 12 |
| Brechin C. | 20 | 4 | 2 | 14 | 10 |

The life and times of a football fan back in the early 70's could be a wee bit different to what we "enjoy" these days. **David Cunningham** relates this wee story about the facilities enjoyed at Hampden at this game, albeit unofficial!

David takes up the story...

*"Well-known Clyde supporter and character Wattie Carruth set up a temporary bar between the Main Stand and the enclosure comprising of a half bottle of whisky and two cans of beer (these were the days when it was permissible to be anaesthetised during a Clyde match!) He gave a multitude of Clyde supporters a drink from the seemingly never-ending half bottle and two cans. On each occasion the story was related in the following months, the number of recipients of drink grew and the event was compared to the Biblical miracle of the loaves and fishes."*

Oh, by the way, Clyde won 3-1!"

*Hampden Park as it was in the early 70's*

## Player Pic – Bobby Harvey                    Gordon Sydney

Bobby Harvey and I had a lot in common when he made his debut in the game against Queens Park; we were both still at school, and we were both making our Hampden debuts.

Injuries to first team players had led to Archie Robertson phoning Bobby, telling him to "bring your boots along to Hampden with you…", and of course Bobby went on to make a scoring debut that day. The best man to describe that goal is Bobby himself…

*"I was over at the main stand side, Clyde were shooting towards the uncovered terracing, and I just hit it as hard as I could then watched it sail past the goalie into the net to open the scoring – what a feeling!"*

My "Hampden debut" also took place "On This Day", and was from the main stand-side enclosure, where I stood as a wide-eyed youngster taking in the (apparent) vastness of the Stadium; and our three goals of course!

But there the similarities end. Bobby stayed as a player with Clyde for another four or five seasons, and I am still here as a Clyde supporter!

Archie Robertson would say of Bobby…"in the modern game Bobby Harvey is a midfield player, but really he's that type of player everyone enjoys watching, a classic Scottish inside-forward, a really clever ball player. Bobby's best season in terms of appearances and goals was 74/75, where he played in just over half the games that season, but still chipped in with eight goals. The first three of those goals came in a game against Airdrie at Shawfield, where Bobby's hat-trick was all that separated Clyde and Airdrie in a league game at Shawfield.

After leaving Clyde in 1978 Bobby went on to play for junior outfits Bellshill Athletic and Renfrew, but that goal at Hampden will always remain one of my cherished childhood memories.

Talking of memories, these days you'll find Bobby heavily involved with the Football Memories Project coordinated by the Scottish Football Museum. There's a class at Hampden…Bobby Harvey…Hampden…memories – it's all coming back to me now!

| DATE | Saturday 6th January 1973 |
|---|---|
| **TOURNAMENT** | League Division Two |
| **FINAL SCORE** | Clyde 4 Queen of the South 1 |
| **TEAM** | *Cairney, Anderson, Swan; Burns, McGoldrick, McHugh;* |
| | *Ahern, Houston, Millar, McGrain and Boyle Sub Thomson* |
| **SCORER(S)** | *Ahern, Boyle, Houston (2)* |
| **ATTENDANCE** | 1667 |
| **REPORTER** | Alan Maxwell |

Clyde had started the New Year with a bang, although at some cost, given the pre-match injury doubts concerning Dom Sullivan, Brian Ahern and Jimmy Burns. In the event, only Dom was ruled out of the starting eleven. Young Bobby Harvey dropped out, and Brian Ahern was moved to the number 7 jersey to replace Dom. John McHugh and Joe McGoldrick were left in the middle of the defence to continue that partnership.

The Bully Wee started this game off in similar vein, Sam Millar crashing a shot off the crossbar from an Ahern corner. It took only eight minutes to open the scoring; some great wing play from Sam Millar saw Peter Boyle crack a shot off the keeper, from which Millar himself was able to force the ball over the line. The goal was disallowed however, in favour of a Clyde penalty, expertly converted by Brian "Fishy" Ahern.

The Bully Wee were flowing, it was no surprise when they added a second on the half hour mark; the visitors keeper fumbled a pass back from player-manager Jim Easton, and up stepped Peter Boyle to take full advantage.

Yet another free-flowing team move allowed Liam Houston to bag a third goal, just on the stroke of half-time. And it was to be big Liam again in the 70th minute to nod home a fourth, and complete the Clyde scoring. A man who would prove to be a thorn in the collective Bully Wee flesh over a long number of years, Tommy Bryce, netted a very late consolation goal for the visitors.

However, there was no doubt after this performance that Clyde were beginning to click in their quest for the Second Division title, with one journalist detailing that "*some of the Clyde players were in a class of their own as they moved the ball about confidently with touches which were a delight to watch*".

## Player Pic – Liam Houston                    Alan Maxwell

A steady and at times spectacular season from young Mr. Houston. Having signed for Clyde from Junior outfit Vale of Leven in the early part of the calendar year, he managed four games in the previous season. Sadly, that fourth game against Morton resulted in a hairline fracture of his leg.

Consequently, he missed a lot of pre-season training, and it was into the early autumn before we started to see the best of Liam's talents. Although signed as an inside-forward, his role, developed by gaffer Archie Robertson, has been mainly defensive, either as a pivot or sweeper. The early season experiment by the gaffer, where Willie McVie was moved up front, and Jimmy Burns brought into centre-half, undoubtedly helped Houston. He was the defensive kingpin, brought in to fill the gap behind the midfield threesome.

Not quite an ever-present, nonetheless, he managed around 40 games, bagging five goals in the process. As a Juvenile, Liam had played in the centre-forward position. He served the team brilliantly in this position, in particular with a couple of very late and crucial counters; equalising in the last minute against Queens Park in September, and an even later equaliser at Central Park Cowdenbeath, as the Bully Wee marched on to Championship success.

Liam was featured in a Match Programme, with "*Mr Consistency*" in the heading. The article continued "*there are very few frills about Liam Houston. He has been assigned a job in the Clyde make-up and carries out that brief to the best of his ability*."

And that standard pleased manager Archie Robertson, who described the form of the tall motor mechanic as "*very consistent this season*."

| | |
|---|---|
| **DATE** | Saturday 13th January 1973 |
| **TOURNAMENT** | League Division Two |
| **FINAL SCORE** | Albion Rovers 0 Clyde 3 |
| **TEAM** | *Cairney, Anderson, Swan; Burns, McGoldrick, McHugh; Ahern, Houston, Millar, McGrain and McGuinness Sub Thomson* |
| **SCORER(S)** | *Ahern, McGuinness, Millar* |
| **ATTENDANCE** | 879 |
| **REPORTER** | Graeme Clark |

Bottom of the table Albion Rovers faced a Clyde team sitting proudly top of the league, but belied their lowly status with a gutsy performance before Clyde, in the end, ran out convincing winners.

Indeed, it was Albion Rovers who were first to threaten when Phil Cairney had to look lively to push a Neil Pirrie shot over for a corner. Clyde settled down after this early scare and McGrain and McGuinness both came close before, in the 35th minute, Ahern was obstructed inside the box. The same player easily converted the resultant spot kick to put Clyde 1 - 0 ahead, a lead they held until half time. The Wee Rovers could have felt aggrieved that they were losing as they had had the better of the half with John Brogan and the lively Pirrie both spurning good opportunities for the home team, drawing good saves from Cairney. It had, in truth though, been a fairly lacklustre first half display from the League leaders.

*Phil Cairney clears his lines during an attack*

That all changed after the break. Clyde clearly had the error of their ways pointed out to them and they moved into top gear, with Rovers having no answer to their slick play, and Clyde were undeniably helped by a goal early in the second half. Rovers impressive trialist keeper did well to parry a fierce drive from Danny McGrain but could do nothing as Eddie McGuinness followed up to net the rebound.

It was all one-way traffic now towards the Rovers goal and the Clyde supporters in the 1,000 crowd were to witness that rarest of things – a missed penalty by Brian Ahern – before Sam Millar headed in an Ahern corner in the 68th minute to put the game beyond Albion Rovers and secure the points for The Bully Wee.

In the end a good win for Clyde, but the first half could have ended with the game already beyond them had they been up against a more clinical opponent. Hopefully a lesson learned!

Archie Robertson praised the players' approach in the way they have accepted and responded to the injury-enforced changes… *"It's most encouraging in the long-term view. They deserve a lot of credit for the way they have tackled their new duties."*

The enforced changes were Dom Sullivan missing three games due to a combination of injury and flu whilst Brian Ahern and Peter Boyle were also out. Jim Burns had stepped out of defence into a midfield role, which allowed John McHugh and Joe McGoldrick to form a partnership in the centre of the defence.

| | P | W | D | L | Pts |
|---|---|---|---|---|---|
| **Clyde** | 22 | 15 | 6 | 1 | 36 |
| Stirling A. | 22 | 14 | 5 | 3 | 33 |
| D'nf'rmlin' | 23 | 14 | 3 | 6 | 31 |
| C'd'nbeath | 24 | 13 | 4 | 7 | 30 |
| St Mirren | 22 | 12 | 4 | 6 | 28 |
| Raith R. | 21 | 11 | 5 | 5 | 27 |
| Montrose | 21 | 10 | 5 | 6 | 25 |
| Q.o.S. | 23 | 9 | 5 | 9 | 23 |
| St'nh's'm'r | 20 | 10 | 2 | 8 | 22 |
| Hamilton | 23 | 9 | 4 | 10 | 22 |
| Berwick R. | 21 | 9 | 3 | 9 | 21 |
| Alloa Ath. | 21 | 6 | 6 | 9 | 18 |
| Stranraer | 22 | 8 | 2 | 12 | 18 |
| Forfar Ath. | 23 | 5 | 6 | 12 | 16 |
| Queen's P. | 23 | 4 | 7 | 12 | 15 |
| E. Stirling | 22 | 5 | 5 | 12 | 15 |
| Brechin C. | 21 | 5 | 2 | 14 | 12 |
| Clydebank | 20 | 5 | 2 | 13 | 12 |
| Albion R. | 22 | 4 | 4 | 14 | 12 |

The league table after this victory was looking healthy, and a useful three-point gap had opened up between Clyde and nearest challengers Stirling Albion.

| | |
|---|---|
| **DATE** | Saturday 20<sup>th</sup> January 1973 |
| **TOURNAMENT** | League Division Two |
| **FINAL SCORE** | Clyde 1 Berwick Rangers 0 |
| **TEAM** | *Cairney, Anderson, Swan; Burns, McGoldrick, McHugh; Ahern, Houston, Millar, McGrain and McGuinness Sub Sullivan (for McGuinness)* |
| **SCORER(S)** | *Burns* |
| **ATTENDANCE** | 1287 |
| **REPORTER** | Alan Maxwell |

This was a game that very nearly didn't take place. As late as the Friday evening before the match, the wee 'Gers had been in touch with the Scottish League in an effort to have the game postponed. Injury and illness had depleted their fourteen-man squad down to just nine fit and available players. Whilst it had been decided to review the situation early in the morning, boss Archie Robertson was busy making tentative arrangements for a friendly fixture with Junior neighbours Cambuslang Rangers whose own League fixture at Greenock looked in some doubt, given the weather affected pitch.

It proved a bit of a false alarm, and it was business as usual at 3.00pm on the Saturday afternoon. When it all got underway, in the middle of a snowstorm, it was hard to believe the guests were injury and illness ravaged, and they probably deserved at least a point for their resolute efforts.

The Bully Wee front line lacked their usual cohesion, it was all a bit "huff and puff". Indeed, it was left to midfield stalwart Jimmy Burns to break the deadlock, and ensure full points to Clyde. If nothing else, the match winner was certainly worth the wait. Jimmy started the move with a free-kick he passed out to Alan Swan. Alan galloped down the left wing, and supplied a swinging cross to the far post, Liam Houston resisted the temptation to blast towards goal; instead he unselfishly pushed the ball back towards the on-rushing Burns, whose magnificent 25-yard left footer was fit to win any game! Clyde were unable to add to their tally, and indeed Berwick had two exceptional chances to grab a point, both of which were surprisingly squandered by striker Ian Hall after impressive probing from Ian Whitehead on both occasions.

If ever there was an example of a team not playing well, but continuing to get the right result, this was it.

And a real bright spot for the Bully Wee faithful was the return of Dom Sullivan, who came on as substitute for Eddie McGuinness in the 55th minute. Our young winger had not enjoyed the best of starts to 1973, having suffered bouts of injury and flu, so it was good to see him ease his way back into the first team.

This result left the league table looking like this...

| | P | W | D | L | Pts |
|---|---|---|---|---|---|
| **Clyde** | **23** | **16** | **6** | **1** | **38** |
| Stirling A. | 22 | 14 | 5 | 3 | 33 |
| D'nf'rmlin' | 23 | 14 | 3 | 6 | 31 |
| C'd'nbeath | 24 | 13 | 4 | 7 | 30 |
| St Mirren | 22 | 12 | 4 | 6 | 28 |
| Raith R. | 22 | 11 | 6 | 5 | 28 |
| Montrose | 22 | 11 | 5 | 6 | 27 |
| St'nh's'm'r | 21 | 11 | 2 | 8 | 24 |
| Q.o.S. | 23 | 9 | 5 | 9 | 23 |
| Hamilton | 23 | 9 | 4 | 10 | 22 |
| Berwick R. | 22 | 9 | 3 | 10 | 21 |
| Alloa Ath. | 21 | 6 | 6 | 9 | 18 |
| Stranraer | 22 | 8 | 2 | 12 | 18 |
| Forfar Ath. | 23 | 5 | 6 | 12 | 16 |
| E. Stirling | 23 | 5 | 6 | 12 | 16 |
| Queen's P. | 23 | 4 | 7 | 12 | 15 |
| Clydebank | 20 | 5 | 2 | 13 | 12 |
| Brechin C. | 22 | 5 | 2 | 15 | 12 |
| Albion R. | 23 | 4 | 4 | 15 | 12 |

| | |
|---|---|
| **DATE** | Saturday 27th January 1973 |
| **TOURNAMENT** | League Division Two |
| **FINAL SCORE** | Clyde 1 Dunfermline Athletic 2 |
| **TEAM** | *Cairney, Anderson, Swan; Burns, McGoldrick, McHugh; Ahern, Houston, Millar, McGrain and McGuinness Sub McVie (for Swan)* |
| **SCORER(S)** | *Burns* |
| **ATTENDANCE** | 3266 |
| **REPORTER** | Graeme Clark |

Clyde went into this match as slight favourites against their fellow promotion challengers, knowing that victory would put them nine points ahead of the Pars as the league entered its final quarter. With just one league defeat all season, allied to a fine win in the earlier corresponding fixture at East End Park, hopes were high down Shawfield way of putting a severe dent in their opponent's title aspirations.

Clyde started the match strongly and Houston was the early sinner when he missed a 7th minute opportunity, but the same player struck just six minutes later to give Clyde what at that time was a deserved lead. Jim Burns was the architect of the goal, sending a slide rule pass through to Houston, who was lurking just outside the penalty box. Liam in turn lashed a rocket of a drive past John Arrol in the Dunfermline goal. Clyde continued to have the edge in the first half with the influential Danny McGrain their midfield mastermind. However, as half time approached Dunfermline were coming more and more into the game, and Phil Cairney had to produce a truly outstanding stop to deny Dave McNicoll and preserve the home team's advantage at the interval. The Fifers had served notice of their intent for the second half.

If Clyde received the notice, they chose to ignore it and paid the penalty. Dunfermline equalised with just four minutes of the second half played, although there was some controversy over the goal. Clyde players claimed that the 25-yard piledriver from Graham Shaw had not crossed the line after thumping down from the bar, but their protestations were in vain and the goal was given by referee Marshall.

This set the tone for the rest of the second half with Dunfermline "upping" their game and Clyde unable to match the renewed graft of their opponents. As a result, Dunfermline continued to press and Clyde were knocked off their usual free flowing stride by their opponent's power play, and it was no great surprise when the visitors went ahead on the hour mark. Left back Jim Wallace latched onto a clearance before storming forward. His cross was perfection for Graham Shaw, who scored his second with a glorious header that beat Phil Cairney all ends up.

Any notion that this setback would revitalise the Bully Wee were soon dashed, as Dunfermline continued to dominate. Indeed, it was the away team who had a great chance to extend their advantage in the 80th minute when Cairney brought down their exciting young striker Ken Mackie in the box for a penalty. Mackie took the spot kick himself but Cairney redeemed himself by saving the striker's effort.

At last Clyde seemed to realise the peril of their situation but the rally was too little too late and although a Houston strike hit the post, Dunfermline held on comfortably to take a fully deserved two points. If there was to be any consolation for the Bully Wee it was that nearest challengers Stirling Albion had also lost at home so Clyde's lead at the top remained at 5 points. The full league table looked like this...

| | P | W | D | L | Pts |
|---|---|---|---|---|---|
| **Clyde** | **24** | **16** | **6** | **2** | **38** |
| D'nf'rmlin' | 24 | 15 | 3 | 6 | 33 |
| Stirling A. | 23 | 14 | 5 | 4 | 33 |
| St Mirren | 23 | 13 | 4 | 6 | 30 |
| Raith R. | 23 | 12 | 6 | 5 | 30 |
| C'd'nbeath | 25 | 13 | 4 | 8 | 30 |
| Montrose | 23 | 12 | 5 | 6 | 29 |
| St'nh's'm'r | 22 | 11 | 2 | 9 | 24 |
| Hamilton | 24 | 10 | 4 | 10 | 24 |
| Q.o.S. | 24 | 9 | 6 | 9 | 24 |
| Berwick R. | 23 | 9 | 3 | 11 | 21 |
| Stranraer | 23 | 9 | 2 | 12 | 20 |
| Alloa Ath. | 22 | 6 | 6 | 10 | 18 |
| E. Stirling | 24 | 6 | 6 | 14 | 18 |
| Forfar Ath. | 24 | 5 | 6 | 13 | 16 |
| Queen's P. | 23 | 4 | 7 | 12 | 15 |
| Clydebank | 21 | 6 | 2 | 13 | 14 |
| Albion R. | 24 | 4 | 5 | 15 | 13 |
| Brechin C. | 23 | 5 | 2 | 16 | 12 |

## Player Pic – John McHugh

*Gordon Sydney*

Successful Second Division campaigns were nothing new to John McHugh!

John had joined Clyde in September 1961, and made his first team debut in January 1962. Clyde were a second division team at the time, however by the end of that season they were promoted as Champions, at the first time of asking.

Unfortunately, our fate the following season was relegation, however once again, in season 63/64, promotion was achieved, although we had to play second-fiddle to Champions Morton that season.

So, season 72/73 was John's third such campaign. At the start of the season he was one of the quartet of players in a contractual dispute with the club, and as such he didn't make his first appearance until late December 1972, when he came on as a substitute for Brian Ahern. Injuries then gave John an extended run in the first team, and his nine-game defensive partnership with Joe McGoldrick yielded five wins, two draws and only two defeats.

Archie Robertson's focus on youth probably restricted John's appearances this season, but, back in the First Division the following season, John's experience proved invaluable and he once again found himself an integral part of the Clyde first team.

In an interview with the Clyde programme for the match v Clydebank in late February, John compared the three Second Division teams he had been part of...

*"**The present Clyde side is better than the Shawfield squad which won the Division Two title in 1961/62, but they are not as good a side as the "Bully***

*Wee" brigade which finished runners-up to Morton two years later – that's because [we] have not reached [our] full potential yet."*

## The Right Record...

On a totally different note (no pun intended!) supporters were advised that the club was about to release a "gramophone record" featuring the players and local folk singer Fraser Bruce. There were two songs called "The Song of the Clyde", and "1-2-3 – Bully Wee for Me", the demo-disc had been sent to London for processing, and copies would be available to purchase in about a month.

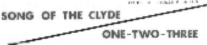

THE CLYDE F.C.

SONG OF THE CLYDE

ONE-TWO-THREE

| | |
|---|---|
| **DATE** | Saturday 3<sup>rd</sup> February 1973 |
| **TOURNAMENT** | Scottish Cup 3<sup>rd</sup> Round |
| **FINAL SCORE** | Clyde 1 Montrose 1 |
| **TEAM** | *Cairney, Anderson, Swan; Burns, McGoldrick, McHugh; Ahern, Houston, Millar, McGrain and Boyle Sub Beattie* |
| **SCORER(S)** | *Millar* |
| **ATTENDANCE** | 1840 |
| **REPORTER** | Jim Hutchison |

This would be the third meeting between the two sides already this season with Clyde winning by the narrowest margin of 1-0 thanks to a Peter Boyle strike in 74 minutes at Links Park, whilst the return league match was even tighter, with Clyde snatching a 2-2 draw thanks to a hotly-disputed penalty in the last minute at Shawfield.

Before the cup tie Archie Robertson emphasised that our main objective was promotion, but that a cup run would be welcome diversion to the "bread-and-butter" of league matches.

This would not be easy against a side who, like ourselves, put the emphasis on attack. Montrose were nine points behind the Bully Wee in the table but they were the league's second top scorers with fifty-six goals scored, seven more than the Bully Wee, and remember this was only the beginning of February!

Clyde tried everything to break down a stubborn Montrose defence but had to be clever at the back themselves as the above statistic was testimony to their forwards prowess.

The sides turned around goalless and again it took Clyde over an hour to finally penetrate the stubborn Gable Endies defence. Ian Thomson, who was on as a substitute from the 37<sup>th</sup> minute for the injured John O'Donnell, blundered and Sam Millar took possession and let fly from distance. George Whisker in the Montrose goal managed to deflect his effort but it just crept in to give Clyde a 71<sup>st</sup> minute lead.

Clyde had the ball in the net again but this time the "goal" was chopped off by the linesman, who inexplicably flagged Peter Boyle offside even though

Montrose had a man on BOTH posts! The great feeling of injustice that the Clyde support in the 1800 strong crowd harboured at this decision was exacerbated when Montrose equalised in the final minute.

Bobby Livingston, easily Montrose's best player, sent a super pass that found the dangerous Brian Third galloping through the middle, and he released a howitzer of a left foot shot from fully thirty yards which flew past the helpless Cairney in the Clyde goal. This took Brian Third's personal goal tally for the season to 24.

Those of you who remember Shawfield Stadium will know that the old ground had one of the longest walks to the dressing room, and the officials were certainly given a hot reception by the stand side patrons as they trudged off the pitch.

So, it would be a replay on the following Wednesday up in Montrose where the fourth meeting of the season would be played out between the sides.

# Aiming for the Charts with Fraser Bruce…

During the course of the season a 7-inch vinyl record was written, recorded and published. It was conceived, organised, written and published by three ardent Clyde fans – Eric Lennon, Joe Kelly and folk singer Fraser Bruce, and it also featured the players singing on it. It was the club's first attempt at Pop Stardom. Fraser Bruce tells the extraordinary story of that attempt by Clyde FC to break into the Pop Business…

"A great friend Joe Kelly, who is sadly no longer with us, was approached by Eric Lennon to see if it was possible to record a "Song of the Clyde". Joe came to me, and it all went from there. Given the three of us were all dedicated Clyde fans it was a "no brainer", so it all began.

I set about writing the lyrics, Eric sorted out the studio, and Joe arranged all the press coverage – we were aiming big!!!!

The original "Song of the Clyde" was written by Ian Gourlay and made popular by Kenneth McKellar, but it wasn't difficult for me to parody the original lyrics, in fact it was a whole lot of fun! Also, not many people realise that the "brilliance" within the song is that every Clyde player that ever won a Scottish Cup medal – whether in 1939, 1955 or 1958 - gets a mention in the song, *and in the actual sequence that they would have been named on the teamsheet*. The only exception to this is Johnny Coyle, who scored the winning goal in 1958.

However, a single has two sides, so a "flip" side song had to be written. Unbelievably, it took less than 15 minutes to write "One, Two, Three". I actually preferred this song because it is chirpy and easy to sing along with, plus it has a lot of humour in it…

> "*Have you ever stood alone wi' a pie up in the stand*
> *Screaming at the Ref as it flies oot o' yer hand*
> *And it hits him in the mouth just before you shouted duck*
> *Well it's just your luck*"

With the songs written Joe, Eric and myself contacted a mutual friend, Jim Poland, and he got a band together which included Ian Gourlay, the man who wrote the original song, who was delighted to be part of it all. I also need to mention Beatrice O'Hara here; we worked together and it was Beatrice that took down the words in shorthand, allowing me to compose as the words came to me.

After only a couple of rehearsals we brought the players in to the recording studios in Bath Street and the songs were recorded.

Was it good? Does it matter? It was cheerful, fun, humorous and it was easy to sing. It also preceded most anthems and may well have been the first 'official' Scottish one, and it seemed to be popular with the fans.

It also travelled the world over. In 1976 I was doing a concert and a radio show way up north in Canada at Yellowknife in the North West Territories. I just about dropped dead when the DJ opened the show playing the Clyde single. He was a Scot and his Clyde-supporting Uncle had sent him a copy as a present. Apparently he played it regularly.

When Clyde moved from Shawfield it did "mess up" the song a bit because some of the references were no longer relevant, and it wasn't until Clyde settled at Broadwood that Eric Lennon and Joe Kelly plucked up the courage to ask me to re-record the songs with the words changed to relate to their current home. It was also an opportunity to change some other lyrics. It was no longer politically correct to say " So I punched her on the jaw and she went hame tae her maw..." so that line, for instance, was changed.

The 'new' CD was a much more professional job and includes Opera singer John Carlo Bellotti plus my brother, professional singer and guitarist Ian Bruce on it. It also includes a third song called "We are a Team", again written by myself, and this latest song is now my favourite because it's a great anthem to sing and wave your arms above your head to. Eric doesn't like it as much because it is down tempo, but the words tell the tales of Clyde's travels around their various "home" venues

Going back to the original pressing, we opted for 750 copies, and they were bought by the Clyde Supporters Club at a cost of 28p plus VAT each. I think we may have sold them for 50p per copy. The single was recorded – ironically – by Thistle Records of Berkeley Street in Glasgow, but they had nothing to do with the football team. Not long after. Partick Thistle did bring out a single, but it was awful!

A little-known fact about "One, Two, Three" is that it was voted Britain's top football anthem by the BBC. The Bryan Burnett show sent a recording crew around the country interviewing all the authors or singers of many of the football anthems in circulation, including the likes of "You'll Never Walk Alone", and we won. We beat them all!

Everybody involved did it for nothing but I was given a special "lifelong admission" award from the club as a "Thank You". I used it once, immediately after receiving it, but I was so embarrassed by the low crowd that I never used it again!

Finally, I used to have a personal copy of the original single, which was signed by all the players, but this has now "disappeared", so if anyone has one they are willing to give away please get in touch..."

*Eddie Anderson (white jersey, centre of picture) holds a copy of the new Clyde FC single. Looking left-to-right you have players Colin Thomson, Willie McVie, Brian Ahern, Joe McGoldrick, Dom Sullivan and Peter Boyle. Clyde supporter and Folk Singer Fraser Bruce is far right, with beard and crew-neck jumper.*

| | |
|---|---|
| **DATE** | Wednesday 7th February 1973 |
| **TOURNAMENT** | Scottish Cup 3rd Round (Replay) |
| **FINAL SCORE** | Montrose 4 Clyde 2 |
| **TEAM** | *Cairney, Anderson, Beattie; Burns, McGoldrick, McHugh; Ahern, Houston, Millar, McGrain and Boyle Sub Thomson (for Houston)* |
| **SCORER(S)** | *Ahern, Houston* |
| **ATTENDANCE** | 2400 |
| **REPORTER** | Jim Hutchison |

This would be the fourth time the sides had met this season, with the previous three fixtures resulting in Clyde having won one, the two others being drawn, so there was no reason to suspect this game would be any different, and a tight affair was predicted. It was virgin territory, though, for at least four of the team – Phil Cairney, Sam Millar, Brian Ahern and Peter Boyle had never played in a Scottish Cup tie before this game!

Clyde started brightly enough and spurned a number of early opportunities, but it was Montrose who struck first through Gordon Crammond in 35 minutes, and Clyde must have felt aggrieved to turn around at half time 0-1 down.

The second half saw Clyde put on a display of non-stop attacking football but as often happens in these situations Montrose took advantage of the inevitable gaps being left at the back and scored a further two goals through breakaways.

First Bobby Livingstone took full advantage of a through ball from Harry Johnston, thus with 76 minutes on the clock Montrose found themselves two up.

Still Clyde chased after the cup tie with real vigour but when Brian Third added a third goal in 85 minutes the home fans were in raptures and must have thought that it was game over!

This Clyde team though never knew when they were beaten and astonishingly scored twice in as many minutes through Brian Ahern and Colin Thomson, who had come on as a sub for Liam Houston.

The taunting gestures to the travelling support, and wide grinning faces of the home fans was now replaced with looks of trepidation, as with score now at

3-2 Clyde threw caution to the wind and everyone was sent up field to try to find an equaliser.

Once again though Montrose broke clear and Gordon Crammond, who had opened the scoring, repeated the trick in the last minute from a Guthrie pass, to finally settle the outcome.

If anyone inside the ground that day had done what an astounding number of football supporters seem to do, and left early, they would have missed four goals in the last five minutes! Now that's what I call a cup tie.

Nevertheless, the outcome was that Clyde were out of the cup and Montrose would face Hamilton Accies at Links Park in the next round.

The only "consolation" was that Clyde could now focus on what Archie Robertson had declared before a ball was kicked that season was top priority - making a return to First Division football within a season.

Goals and Gable Ends, a history of Montrose FC by Forbes Inglis, similarly enthused about the replay…

*"The replay…attracted 2400 to Links Park for one of the most remarkable cup-ties the ground would ever stage. With five minutes left, Montrose were leading 3-0 after an attacking performance that had the Wellington Street enclosure singing their heads off. Then Clyde scored twice in the 87th and 88th minute to stun Montrose. Just when it looked like a panic-ridden Montrose collapse was on the cards, Guthrie and Crammond combined for the latter to score and relieve the pressure on the pitch and the terraces."*.

## Player Pic – Colin Thomson                    Alan Maxwell

Colin was signed from Kirkintilloch Rob Roy late in 1970, and it didn't take him long to establish himself as a "Robertson Babe". Skilful, with an excellent footballing brain, and scoring regular goals in the reserve team, he quickly persuaded gaffer Robertson to give him a start.

His debut came in a midweek tussle at Tannadice against Dundee United. Sadly, he was to have little influence on this one; Clyde losing out to the only goal of the evening. Not all bad though, he did enough to retain his place in the side for the remaining four games of the season. This was not a good time to be making a debut for Clyde, all five of those end of season fixtures resulted in defeat. Indeed, the famous Bully Wee didn't manage another League victory after beating Falkirk 3-2 at the Academy on Boxing Day 1970.

Colin made an immediate impact at the start of the next season, bagging Clyde's only goal in a 1-4 loss to Gillingham, in our first pre-season friendly fixture. He was to feature mainly with the reserve team, netting 7 goals prior to Christmas. The signing of Joe McBride was the catalyst for improvement in Thomson's fortunes. McBride had an immediate impact and the main beneficiary was Colin. With his agile brain, he immediately struck up a fruitful partnership, and managed to string a few consecutive games, scoring the winner in a festive match against Dunfermline Athletic.

He featured intermittently throughout this Championship season, with 9 appearances and 3 goals, importantly contributing in the last few games as we grasped the Title, but unfortunately his two goals in our very last game of the season against St Mirren couldn't save him from being released.

| | |
|---|---|
| **DATE** | Saturday 10th February 1973 |
| **TOURNAMENT** | League Division Two |
| **FINAL SCORE** | Raith Rovers 0 Clyde 0 |
| **TEAM** | *Cairney, Anderson, Burns; Beattie, McGoldrick, McHugh; Ahern, Thomson, Millar, McGrain and Boyle Sub Sullivan (for Boyle)* |
| **ATTENDANCE** | 2995 |
| **REPORTER** | Graeme Clark |

Sadly, this game was the very epithet of the no-score draw, a dull and drab affair, a contest dominated by the defences on both sides. Clyde, in particular, seemed determined to settle for a draw from the outset against a team on the fringes of the promotion battle, some 8 points behind league leaders the Bully Wee, although with a game in hand.

Raith took the game to Clyde from the outset, forcing a corner in the very first minute that came to nothing. Cairney was the first of the keepers to be called into action when he brilliantly parried a close range shot from Joe Baker after 17 minutes. The rebound fell to the same player, and this time his follow up was cleared off the line by Eddie Anderson. It would be another 17 minutes before the Clyde goal was troubled again and once more it was the ex-England Internationalist Baker causing the problem, this time his header scraping a post on the way past. In between times, Clyde were rarely seen as an attacking force although McGrain and Beattie did have shots at goal which did not really trouble the home keeper.

The second half was much of the same dreary fare to the chagrin of the 3000 or so paying punters inside Starks Park. The only real talking point in this stalemate was a Robertson lob that landed on the top of the Clyde net. Clyde brought on Sullivan on 65 minutes in an attempt to bring their performance to life but to no avail. As the half wore on Raith seemed to accept that one point each was the order of the day and so the game petered out to its inevitable conclusion.

Clyde's best performances came in defence as you might imagine, with Cairney, Burns, McGoldrick and McHugh all turning in sterling displays.

*Action pic from Kirkcaldy...Eddie Anderson leaps high, Phil Cairney is poised to take the high ball, and Joe McGoldrick looks on.*

All in all, a game best forgotten but a valuable point all the same for Clyde in the race to the flag.

And Archie Robertson was satisfied!

" ***This was a good point. We knew this would be a difficult one, especially in view of the recent upsets against Dunfermline and Montrose. Undoubtedly, we missed players like Dom Sullivan and Alan Swan in these games, but a word of credit is due Jimmy Burns for the versatility shown by stepping to full-back to take over from Alan Swan.***"

Meanwhile, **Jim Hutchison** recounts the tale of a defender who wouldn't give in*....*

"*I vividly recall Joe McGoldrick playing up at Starks Park and after a clash of heads he had a severe mouth injury - broken or lost teeth, I think. Anyway, in the days before multiple subs Big Joe was patched up and sent back on with a sponge stuck in his mouth! As the game progressed this got bloodier and bloodier until the poor guy was resembling a plastic duck! No "mamby-pamby-must change your shirt" in those days - big Joe just had to carry on, Aye men were men then, no rolling about on the turf or simulation in those days.*"

## Player Pic – Joe McGoldrick                    **Alan Maxwell**

An interesting season for young Joseph, who celebrated his 21st birthday during the course of the campaign. He was the only outfield player not to register at least one goal as Clyde strove towards the Championship Title. In the words of skipper **Danny McGrain** though, he proved a reliable defender who managed 20 games at the heart of the defence..."*good in the air, and composed on the ground*", Joe became "Mr. Reliable", most especially in the second half of the season.

Having signed as a youngster from St Mirens BG in September 1969, it took Joe the best part of three years to make an impression. "Inconsistency, lack of command and unsteadiness in the air", were all criticisms of his early years, but refreshingly, these were Joe's own comments.

John McHugh in particular must take credit for the marked improvement of this young centre-half..."*I've got to thank Mike Clinton, Willie McVie and John McHugh, they worked specifically with me in training*", quoted the much-improved Joe, however the healthy partnership with McHugh was developed in both reserve and friendly games, and with their introduction to first team duty, the Bully Wee instantly became that bit harder to beat. In nine games, they only conceded ten goals, and if you ignore the four goals lost at Montrose in the Cup replay, a more realistic tally is less than a-goal-a-game.

Joe was to depart the Shawfield scene in 1974, after 70 games, with sadly never a goal to his name!

| | |
|---|---|
| **DATE** | Tuesday 20th February 1973 |
| **TOURNAMENT** | League Division Two |
| **FINAL SCORE** | Clyde 4 Brechin City 1 |
| **TEAM** | *Cairney, Anderson, Burns; McHugh, McGoldrick, Ahern, Sullivan, Thomson, Millar, McGrain and Boyle Sub Beattie (for Thomson)* |
| **SCORER(S)** | *Ahern (2), Beattie (2)* |
| **ATTENDANCE** | 1104 |
| **REPORTER** | Jim Hutchison |

This match was originally scheduled to have been played on Saturday the 17th of February, but postponement due to the weather delayed it until Tuesday the 20th of February. As Clyde fans approached this rearranged game, our 26th in the league, some supporters were getting a bit nervous, wondering if the wheels were coming off our title charge. Clyde's Scottish Cup adventure had ended ten days earlier after a replay away against Montrose and after a gruelling match in Kirkcaldy the previous Saturday when Clyde drew 0-0 it was time to get back on winning ways.

The first half in all truth was a shocker by both sides, Clyde had taken the lead in the 22nd minute with what could best be described as a speculative 25-yard effort from Brian Ahern, which somehow Andy McEwan in the Brechin goal allowed to slip through his hands and give the Bully Wee the lead.

In what was becoming a nightmare for the keepers the usually very reliable Phil Cairney was badly at fault 12 minutes later when a Jim Donnelly lob completely deceived him and hit the bar, rebounding to a delighted Geoff Coutts to nod into the empty net to level the scores at 1-1, and that is how the first half ended.

Ten minutes into the second half Archie Robertson had clearly seen enough and replaced number 8 Colin Thomson with substitute Billy Beattie.

It proved to be yet another masterstroke by our manager as eight minutes later, prompted by the aggressive Beattie, Clyde roared into attack and Danny McGrain was bundled to the ground by Miller of Brechin, and from the resultant penalty Brian Ahern put Clyde back into the lead in 63 minutes.

Three minutes later Billy Beattie scored a peach of a goal when he galloped forward onto a beautiful Dom Sullivan flicked pass and crashed home a tremendous right foot shot from all of 25 yards to put the Bully Wee 3-1 in front.

With time running out McGrain found himself in the penalty area again, this time he pivoted and unleashed a great shot that McEwan did well to block, but that man Beattie was right on the spot to prod home his second and Clyde's fourth in the 86th minute.

| | P | W | D | L | Pts |
|---|---|---|---|---|---|
| Clyde | 26 | 17 | 7 | 2 | 41 |
| Dunfermline | 25 | 16 | 3 | 6 | 35 |
| Stirling Albion | 24 | 15 | 5 | 4 | 35 |
| St Mirren | 26 | 14 | 5 | 7 | 33 |
| Raith Rovers | 24 | 12 | 7 | 5 | 31 |
| Montrose | 25 | 13 | 5 | 7 | 31 |
| Cowdenbeath | 26 | 13 | 5 | 8 | 31 |
| Hamilton Acas. | 26 | 11 | 5 | 10 | 27 |
| Stenhousemuir | 24 | 11 | 4 | 9 | 26 |
| Queen of South | 25 | 9 | 6 | 10 | 24 |
| Berwick Ran. | 24 | 10 | 3 | 11 | 23 |
| Stranraer | 24 | 10 | 2 | 12 | 22 |
| Alloa Athletic | 24 | 7 | 7 | 10 | 21 |
| Queen's Park | 26 | 6 | 8 | 12 | 20 |
| East Stirling | 26 | 6 | 6 | 14 | 18 |
| Forfar Athletic | 27 | 5 | 8 | 14 | 18 |
| Clydebank | 23 | 6 | 3 | 14 | 15 |
| Albion Rovers | 26 | 4 | 5 | 17 | 13 |
| Brechin City | 25 | 5 | 2 | 18 | 12 |

With the game well and truly over Brechin's Dave Cunningham was ordered off in the last minute for a wild challenge on Danny McGrain to complete a night of misery for the Glebe Park side, leaving them rock bottom of the table a mere twenty-nine points adrift of the Shawfield league leaders, who were now six points clear at the top.

Another favourite son Jimmy Rowan, who had been scouting for Celtic, returned to Shawfield for the third time in his career having played with Clyde in the 50's and returning in the 60's, this time to take over coaching duties from Mike Clinton who had given up the post due to other commitments outside of football.

## Player Pic – Billy Beattie                              Alan Maxwell

Signed in late 1968, Billy was a tenacious wing half, equally comfortable whether playing in defence or further forward as a midfielder of some note.

He was famously – or infamously – sent off against Airdrie in the last game of season 71/72, the match that relegated us, but he will forever argue that his tackle was never a sending-off!

Regardless, his impressive performances in midfield earned him rave reviews that season (71/72), but it was as a defensive sweeper that Manager Archie Robertson thought Billy was best suited. Given the strength of the 72/73 team defensively, it was going to be difficult for Billy to claim a regular starting position. Despite that, Billy still managed to make ten starts during the season, scoring a creditable five goals. These included a double in the 4 – 1 home win over Brechin City, a match which turned in Clyde's favour after Billy was introduced as a second half substitute.

When he left Clyde, Billy tried his luck with Durban United in South Africa. When he returned to these shores in the late 70's, following a brief spell in the juniors with Ballieston, Billy went senior again with Forfar Athletic for a couple of seasons. He wound down his career with East Kilbride Thistle and Kilsyth Rangers.

100

| | |
|---|---|
| **DATE** | Saturday 24th February 1973 |
| **TOURNAMENT** | League Division Two |
| **FINAL SCORE** | Clyde 1 Clydebank 0 |
| **TEAM** | *Cairney, Anderson, Burns; Houston, McGoldrick, Ahern,* |
| | *Sullivan, Beattie, Millar, McGrain and Boyle Sub McVie* |
| **SCORER(S)** | *Millar* |
| **ATTENDANCE** | 1403 |
| **REPORTER** | Gordon Sydney |

Whilst the history books will record that the Bully Wee beat this latest reincarnation of Clydebank FC, took the points and consolidated their position at the top of the league, the story of the match itself doesn't make pleasant reading - "the sort of game that would make spectators stay at home" was one journalist's summation.

As a mere youngster, probably not yet into double-figures in terms of attendance at Clyde matches, I don't remember that much about the game. What I do remember is Sam Millar strolling through towards the goal at the Tote end and sliding the ball home, ultimately for the only goal of the game. We were in the Stand pretty much in line with the penalty box, so all was well as far as I was concerned. I'm sure I also remember Dom Sullivan sending a high, looping cross from his right-wing berth into the Tote-end goalmouth, whereupon it hit the top of the bar and bounced back into play – amazing stuff to this young and impressionable eight-year-old!

Older, wiser, sages – those that are usually employed by newspapers, who sometimes seem to have a monopoly on them - summed matters up differently. The match was apparently a let-down in terms of entertainment and performance. Clyde's "wild shooting and poor passing" was what one journalist partially blamed it on, however he levelled up his accusations by describing a packed Bankies defence, and their mastery of the offside trap, as providing "dull, negative and boring football".

Jim Burns set up the only goal of the game in the fifteenth minute. A harmless looking ball into the box looked as if it would be easily gathered by Bankies keeper Gallagher, however he got it completely wrong, and, as previously described, allowed Sam Millar to easily pick his spot and score up at the Tote end.

Phil Cairney might "have been embarrassed to ask for wages" such was his lack of action in the first half, however when called into action just a minute before the break he threw himself across the goal to turn away a net bound shot from Billy McColl, yet another player from this Division that would later play for the Bully Wee.

Clyde continued to have most of the game, but by then it had become bogged down in a congested midfield, with Clydebank seemingly intent on pursuing a damage-limitation strategy. Archie Robertson brought Willie McVie on in place of Liam Houston to bolster the forward line, but still no further goals came for either team.

In the end, Clyde won the match, kept a clean sheet, consolidated pole position in the league, and we all – especially this youngster - went home happy.

What is there not to like about a Clyde victory?

*Joe McGoldrick, Dom Sullivan and Jim Burns*

| | |
|---|---|
| **DATE** | Saturday 3<sup>rd</sup> March 1973 |
| **TOURNAMENT** | League Division Two |
| **FINAL SCORE** | Stranraer 1 Clyde 2 |
| **TEAM** | *Cairney, Anderson, Burns; Houston, McGoldrick, Ahern,* |
| | *Sullivan, Beattie, Millar, McGrain and Boyle Sub McVie* |
| **SCORER(S):** | *Sullivan, Own Goal* |
| **ATTENDANCE** | 1152 |
| **REPORTER** | Alan Maxwell |

Table-topping Clyde were keen to ensure a profitable return from the South West of the country, and the cause was certainly helped by a bit of a whirlwind start. Right from the off, the home defence was in some disarray, and within two minutes both Heap and Whiteside were spoken to by referee Webster, both having shown dissent at a free kick decision.

It was to be Dom Sullivan who would settle Bully Wee nerves with an opener after just seven minutes. A typical Dom move, he took a throw-in, received the ball back, beat a couple of home defenders, shifted the ball to his left foot and hammered beyond the helpless Willie Whiteside in the home goal.

But Clyde were conceding too many free-kicks, and it was to prove their downfall after twenty minutes. Following a twice-taken indirect free-kick, Billy Collings squared to Davie Booth who drove home to equalise. Phil Cairney had been injured earlier, when he collided with an upright and it appeared this may have prevented him from stopping Booth's shot. It was end-to-end for the rest of the first half. Whiteside had a brilliant save from a Millar header, whilst at the other end Cairney missed a cross ball, leaving Booth a seemingly simple task to head home into an empty net, but miraculously Eddie Anderson popped up to make a crucial goal line clearance.

The Bully Wee were to start the second half in the same whirlwind fashion. After just two minutes, a Sullivan cross was deflected into his own net by defender Heap. The home team pressed desperately for the rest of the half, and Clyde found themselves frustrated to such an extent they conceded a significant number of fouls, but eventually, when Billy Beattie found his name in the wee black book, it was for time-wasting.

Gaffer Archie Robertson was delighted with the final outcome. Although the team had not been firing on all cylinders in recent weeks the value of teamwork nurtured by the Boss was helping to stack up the points, even though the performances had slipped when compared with the earlier part of the season.

Although Dom Sullivan had been struggling with a troublesome groin injury, his inspired performance, where he linked up brilliantly with Brian Ahern, would prove to be instrumental as Clyde pushed on towards Championship glory.

| | P | W | L | D | Pts |
|---|---|---|---|---|---|
| **Clyde** | **28** | **19** | **2** | **7** | **45** |
| Dunfermline | 27 | 18 | 6 | 3 | 39 |
| St Mirren | 28 | 15 | 7 | 6 | 36 |
| Stirling | 25 | 15 | 5 | 5 | 35 |
| Raith Rovers | 26 | 14 | 5 | 7 | 35 |
| Cowdenbeath | 28 | 14 | 9 | 5 | 33 |
| Montrose | 25 | 13 | 7 | 5 | 31 |
| Hamilton | 27 | 12 | 10 | 5 | 29 |
| Stenhousem'r | 26 | 11 | 9 | 6 | 28 |
| Berwick | 26 | 11 | 12 | 3 | 25 |
| Q.O.S. | 30 | 9 | 12 | 6 | 24 |
| Alloa | 27 | 8 | 11 | 8 | 24 |
| Stranraer | 25 | 10 | 13 | 2 | 22 |
| Queens Park | 27 | 7 | 12 | 8 | 22 |
| East Stirling | 28 | 7 | 14 | 1 | 21 |
| Forfar | 29 | 5 | 16 | 8 | 18 |
| Albion Rovers | 28 | 5 | 17 | 6 | 16 |
| Clydebank | 26 | 6 | 17 | 3 | 15 |
| Brechin | 27 | 5 | 20 | 2 | 12 |

| **DATE** | Saturday 10th March 1973 |
|---|---|
| **TOURNAMENT** | League Division Two |
| **FINAL SCORE** | Clyde 0 Hamilton Accies 0 |
| **TEAM** | *Cairney, Anderson, Burns; Houston, McGoldrick, Ahern, Sullivan, Beattie, Millar, McGrain and Boyle Sub McVie* |
| **ATTENDANCE** | 3021 |
| **REPORTER** | Graeme Clark |

Although Clyde held a healthy lead at the top of the table going into this clash, they were facing an Accies team who could claim to be the form side in the league since the turn of the year, having taken 12 points from a possible 14 in their last 7 games.

In the event, the teams couldn't be separated as they played out an entertaining goalless draw, allowing Hamilton to stretch their unbeaten run further into 1973.

Clyde started the brighter of the two teams. Brian Ahern had the first chance of the game, but watched in frustration as his drive went just wide of McLean's goal. Accies hit back and Ahern was involved again, this time in defence as he cleared a Young centre for a corner, with future Clyde legend Neil Hood waiting to pounce.

Both keepers were at their best in the game, with McLean in the Accies goal having the pick of the saves when he tipped away a Millar thunderbolt. McLean thwarted the same player for a second time when he held his ambitious attempt from a bicycle kick. Houston then went close for Clyde with a piledriver from a Sullivan corner that flew inches past the post, but it was Hamilton who almost snatched the lead when Lawless split the Clyde defence with a precision pass to Hegarty. Hegarty then found Hood with just Cairney to beat, but the Clyde keeper rose to the occasion, blocking the big centre's effort before Jim Burns completed the clearance.

The second half saw more of the same with both teams creating and spurning chances. McLean easily gathered an Ahern shot before Anderson popped up on the line to clear a goal-bound Hegarty header and prevent the away side from taking the lead. As the second half progressed it was the Accies who looked the stronger of the two teams, and the Clyde defence was coming under more pressure. Cairney again denied Hood, kicking away from the onrushing centre forward, then Houston almost put through his own goal with a dodgy pass back. In the end however, the respective defences won out, although this was by no means a dull match, with a draw just about right over the 90 minutes as a whole.

An interesting footnote to the game concerned Peter Boyle who had one of his quieter shifts, but perhaps his mind was on the forthcoming big midweek match, that is to say his wedding!

*Peter Boyle attempts to go around the Accies defence but future Clyde player Gordon Hamilton clears.*

| | |
|---|---|
| **DATE** | Saturday 17th March 1973 |
| **TOURNAMENT** | League Division Two |
| **FINAL SCORE** | Stenhousemuir 1 Clyde 2 |
| **TEAM** | *Carr, Anderson, Burns; Houston, McGoldrick, Ahern, Sullivan, McVie, Millar, McGrain and Boyle Sub Swan (for McGoldrick)* |
| **SCORER(S)** | *McVie, Anderson* |
| **ATTENDANCE** | 754 |
| **REPORTER** | Jim Hutchison |

One of my main memories of this game was that it was getting to what Sir Alex Ferguson was many years later to describe as "squeaky bum time". As I climbed aboard the old Rutherglen & Burnside Supporters bus that day, as far as I can recall the main topic of conversation was how would the new goalie, brought in to replace Phil Cairney at this important point of the run-in to the championship, perform? Without the mass of information available these days, we knew very little about Neil Carr. Only that he was only 19, and was now the fourth-choice goalkeeper for Celtic as Celtic had signed Ally Hunter who was in line for Scotland's No 1 shirt from Kilmarnock in the January, and he was vying for the first team slot with Evan Williams and Denis Connaghan. Interestingly, the latter two goalkeepers would eventually follow in Neil Carr's footsteps and play between the sticks at Shawfield.

So, what was this youngster like then? On arrival at Ochilview it was not an inspiring figure that emerged in the Clyde's custodian's jersey. Neil, in those days, was slightly built, a "tall youngster" was the more polite description, but the more forthright opinion was of a skinny gangling kid with not so much the physique of a Greek God but more like a kebab stick!

What had Archie Robertson been thinking of to sign him?

Stenhousemuir had of course handed us our first defeat at Shawfield by three goals to one earlier in the season; the supporters were still smarting from this and were hoping for a bit of revenge for this previous reverse.

Stenhousemuir went ahead after only twenty minutes through a Wight goal, the same man who had scored from the spot at Shawfield in the earlier fixture. Although it could not be blamed in any way on the keeper, it could have spelt disaster for young Neil's debut and set up Stenny for a double over us.

If the nerves among the support were tangible it in no way transposed itself onto the park and to our new keeper, who had a storming game with three splendid saves in the remainder of the first half from Henderson, Murdoch and Rose to keep Clyde only one down at the interval.

So, what is it they say, never judge a book by its cover; fair to say the youngster was keeping Clyde in the match!

We don't know what Archie said at the interval but whatever it was it worked as the Clyde team got its act together and came storming back, dominating the second half and scoring two goals in a minute. Equalising through big Willie McVie in the 54th minute, we immediately went up the park again and Eddie Anderson, our stalwart right back, cracked in the winner less than sixty seconds later - indeed both goals were recorded by the press as the 54th minute.

Eddie rarely appeared on the scoresheet for Clyde, as he seldom strayed from his defensive duties. It was rumoured that he got a nose bleed or altitude sickness if he went too far up the park! So, a rare item indeed, but nevertheless very warmly greeted by the Clyde faithful, as this meant Clyde were still unbeaten away from home. A seven-point gap had now opened up between us and our nearest rivals Dunfermline Athletic, who lost 1-2 at Douglas Park whilst we were beating Stenhousemuir by the same scoreline. Although they had a game in hand, with Clyde only having six games left and only two points for a win in those days, a bit of breathing space was opening up in our run in to the finishing line and the title.

| | P | W | L | D | Pts |
|---|---|---|---|---|---|
| Clyde | 30 | 20 | 2 | 8 | 48 |
| Dunfermline | 29 | 19 | 7 | 3 | 41 |
| Stirling A. | 28 | 17 | 6 | 5 | 39 |
| Raith Rov. | 28 | 16 | 5 | 7 | 39 |
| St. Mirren | 29 | 16 | 7 | 6 | 38 |
| Cowdenbeath | 30 | 14 | 10 | 6 | 34 |
| Montrose | 26 | 13 | 7 | 6 | 32 |
| Hamilton | 29 | 13 | 10 | 6 | 32 |
| Berwick R. | 28 | 13 | 12 | 3 | 29 |
| Stenh'sem'r | 28 | 11 | 11 | 6 | 28 |
| Q.O.S. | 28 | 19 | 12 | 6 | 26 |
| Alloa | 28 | 8 | 12 | 8 | 24 |
| E. Stirling | 30 | 8 | 15 | 7 | 23 |
| Queen's Park | 27 | 7 | 12 | 8 | 22 |
| Stranraer | 28 | 10 | 16 | 2 | 22 |
| Forfar | 29 | 5 | 16 | 8 | 18 |
| Clydebank | 28 | 7 | 18 | 3 | 17 |
| Albion R. | 29 | 5 | 18 | 6 | 16 |
| Brechin | 28 | 5 | 21 | 2 | 12 |

These days, players can be credited for an "assist", as well as actually scoring the goal. If that criteria had been applied back in 72/73, would Peter Boyle have been able to claim an "assist" at this game? *Jim Hutchison* puts forward his case...

*"I remember standing behind the goal at Stenhousemuir, where in those days you were close enough to have some great banter with the players, in this case wee Peter Boyle. He was winding up Stewart Kennedy, who was at that time the Stenny keeper, before he went to Rangers. Wee Peter was pulling his shirt and chirping away at him and so distracted was he that he missed the ball coming in from the corner and Clyde scored. He was livid as I recall! Mind you not as livid as I was when some years later I travelled to Wembley and he had a nightmare for Scotland!"*

Meanwhile, people on the terracing of Second Division grounds maybe turned out differently to what they were thought to be for one Clyde supporter, as *David Cunningham* relates...

*"On a visit to Ochilview, one of the locals engaged us in conversation. He asked if there were any Clyde players he should particularly look out for. I was singing the praises of Dom Sullivan and Danny McGrain when I realised that he was taking notes – he was a local reporter who probably went directly to the pub having done his afternoon's work!"*

*Scoreflash...Willie all but settles matters...Willie McVie 6 Danny McGrain 2...*

| | |
|---|---|
| **DATE** | Saturday 24<sup>th</sup> March 1973 |
| **TOURNAMENT** | League Division Two |
| **FINAL SCORE** | Clyde 1 East Stirling 1 |
| **TEAM** | *Carr, Anderson, Swan; Houston, Burns, Ahern; Sullivan, McVie, Millar, McGrain and Boyle Sub Thomson* |
| **SCORER(S)** | *Boyle* |
| **ATTENDANCE** | 1353 |
| **REPORTER** | Gordon Sydney |

With Neil Carr keeping his place in goal, and Alan Swan back to his now-customary left back role, confidence was there that two points could be garnered at the expense of East Stirling, a team that we had humbled on their own ground earlier in the season.

But football isn't played on paper, and it took until the hour-mark for the deadlock to be broken, Peter Boyle's head directing a Brian Ahern cross into the net.

Before that, it was a series of missed chances for the Bully Wee; Peter Boyle hit the outside of the net with a shot, then both he and Sam Millar failed to connect with Dom Sullivan's cross. The role was reversed shortly afterwards, when Dom got his foot to Peter's cross, only to see it fly over the crossbar. In a forerunner of the goal, a Brian Ahern cross was met by Peter's head, but he only succeeded in putting his header right into keeper Bert Archibald's grasp. There was still time before the break for the relatively unlikely pairing of Willie McVie and Liam Houston to work their way through the away defence, but Liam didn't make the most of the pass from Willie to bring the move to a close. Finally, after a frenetic first half, Willie McVie's cross gave both Sam Millar and Peter Boyle the opportunity to take a shot, but both shots were blocked.

It wasn't all one-way traffic, and for a spell in that first half the Clyde defence struggled to contain the East Stirling forwards. As if that wasn't warning enough, just four minutes into the second half Jim McPaul found himself right in on goal, but he miskicked, allowing Neil Carr the chance to save – albeit in a most unorthodox fashion – using his foot.

Normal service resumed, with Sullivan having a couple of shots saved before Peter Boyle got that header and put us ahead – his first goal since early January.

Despite continuing to press, with only one goal in it there was always the chance of East Stirling grabbing an equaliser, and so it proved. Four minutes from the end Liam Houston pulled down Jim McPaul in the box, Ian Browning equalised from the spot, and that was how the match finished.

## A Record...

Danny McGrain, Brian Ahern and John McHugh were given a sneak listen to the new Clyde FC single by Fraser Bruce. Pre-release orders were being taken, and sales figures were already looking positive...

## John Watson

John Watson, who would make the Clyde physio position his own for many a long year, joined the club this season.

## Player Pic – Eddie Anderson                    Graeme Clark

Eddie Anderson was the epitome of the loyal Club servant. Born in 1949, Eddie joined Clyde from Kirkintilloch Rob Roy in 1969, making his name as a rugged, no nonsense full back with the Bully Wee over the next 11 years, leaving the Club in 1980. In that time, he played some 292 league games, chipping in with 5 goals. In his Clyde career, a host of other games took his appearances to over 360, and his goal "haul" to six - so an Eddie Anderson goal was a rare sight indeed. And, of course, he was an integral part of two Second Division Championship-winning teams, in 1972/73 and 1977/78.

Eddie was not a tall man, just 5' 9", weighing in at 11st 6lbs, but as a right back he was tenacious, and forged a formidable full back pairing in this season with Alan Swan. Like his team mates, Eddie had a job away from football – working with the Post Office as an Electrician at the time.

1972/73 was perhaps his most successful, not to mention eventful, season at the Club. Following the pay revolt by certain of the more experienced players, Eddie, at the age of 23, incredibly found himself as "elder statesman" of the team, along with Willie McVie, and he responded magnificently, finding a level of consistency that had eluded him the previous season when he had been in and out of the team. His reward was to be one of only two ever-presents in the season, and the only defender to appear in all competitive matches.

He even managed a goal, scoring the winner in a 2-1 victory away to Stenhousemuir, a match that saw the first appearance on the bench of long-time Club Physio John Watson. Indeed, the only thing Eddie missed all season was the official photo shoot for the launch of the Fraser Bruce single, Song of the Clyde. He was getting married that day, so perhaps understandable!

| | |
|---|---|
| **DATE** | Saturday 31st March 1973 |
| **TOURNAMENT** | League Division Two |
| **FINAL SCORE** | Stirling Albion 3 Clyde 1 |
| **TEAM** | *Carr, Anderson, Swan; Houston, Burns; Ahern; Sullivan, McVie, Millar, McGrain and Boyle Sub Thomson* |
| **SCORER(S)** | *Ahern* |
| **ATTENDANCE** | 2394 |
| **REPORTER** | Alan Maxwell |

Having gone through the season to date unbeaten on their travels, the Bully Wee were confident of extending that run against a Stirling side who saw themselves in the "last chance" saloon. Clyde were firm favourites for the title, sitting with 49 points from 31 games. Albion had amassed 41 points but had two games in hand over their visitors. With the Fife duo of Raith Rovers and Dunfermline Athletic still well placed, the home outfit really had to end that proud Clyde record.

This was very much a game of two halves for the Clyde faithful to digest. First half saw a strong confident Clyde side play some of their best football in the calendar year. Just a modicum of luck could have seen the game out of Stirling's reach before the interval. Sammy Millar seemed to have broken the deadlock after 15 minutes, but was adjudged offside. No matter, just a few minutes later and Fishy was to open the scoring, for real this time; he scattered the home defence with a penetrating run and finished it all off with a powerful drive past a helpless Young from ten yards.

Alas it was a short-lived lead. Just two minutes later and centre-forward McMillan converted a cross from an old Clyde adversary, Mickey Lawson, leaving keeper Neil Carr with no chance. Worse was to follow, Lawson turned goal taker on the half hour mark, blasting a free-kick from Clyde-supporter Andy Stevenson into the net from 20 yards.

Clyde were shell-shocked to find themselves in arrears at the interval, despite completely dominating the first forty-five minutes. Albion had managed a number of last gasp goal line clearances.

Things looked better for the Bully Wee when goal scorer McMillan was sent off on the hour mark, and correctly so, for a foul on Eddie Anderson, a second bookable offence. But despite this loss, Albion maintained the advantage, and continued to take the game to Clyde. Pushing frantically with a late surge the Bully Wee could not find that elusive equaliser, and "sods law" intervened in the third minute of injury time when McPhee grabbed a third and decisive goal for the Albion.

All in all, this was a torrid fixture, a first and only away defeat, in a match where they had contributed so much. With hindsight, we might have realised this would not be our afternoon, upon production of the Home team lines. Appearing at left-back in place of the injured McAleer, and worthy of special mention, "Terry Christie, the veteran played a prominent part in his team's win and had a remarkably fine game considering this was only his second appearance in the League side this season"

Would you believe it, even away back then, Mr Christie ruining a Saturday night for the Bully Wee faithful!

*Annfield, Stirling Albion's home ground in the 70's*

| DATE | Saturday 7th April 1973 |
|---|---|
| TOURNAMENT | League Division Two |
| FINAL SCORE | Cowdenbeath 1 Clyde 1 |
| TEAM | *Carr, Anderson, Swan; Burns, Houston, Ahern; Sullivan, Paterson, Millar, McGrain and Boyle Sub McGoldrick* |
| SCORER(S) | *Houston* |
| ATTENDANCE | 1242 |
| REPORTER | Alan Maxwell |

Having lost their first away fixture at Stirling Albion, the previous Saturday, this tough visit to Central Park was sure to fully test the resolve of a wounded Bully Wee side unused to such ignominy. Pre-match the big talking point for the Bully Wee faithful headed east was the likely inclusion of centre-forward Billy Paterson. The striker had signed on a short-term loan to assist gaffer Robertson get over the injury crisis affecting the top end of his side. Vastly experienced, Billy had played in both recent Junior Cup Finals for his parent club Cambuslang Rangers.

Paterson was indeed chosen to lead the line. Things were looking pretty bleak when the Fifers snatched an early lead through Laing. Clyde's prospects seemed to improve as 'Beath were only able to send out ten men for the second half. However, in a similar vein to the previous Saturday when they were incapable of overcoming a ten-man team, we were unable to penetrate a human barricade of home defenders.

Cometh the hour, cometh the man, and up stepped stalwart Liam Houston to net from close range with just the three minutes remaining on the clock. It was all getting very tight at the top. Clyde now led by four points, with three games remaining. However, there was a bit to go, as they were closely chased by Dunfermline and Stirling Albion, both with games in hand. Something would inevitably give a few days later, as the challengers were due to meet midweek in the catch-up fixture. As for Mr. Paterson, well famously this was to prove his only game in Clyde colours!

|  | P | W | D | L | Pts |
|---|---|---|---|---|---|
| **Clyde** | 33 | 20 | 10 | 3 | 50 |
| Dunfermline | 32 | 21 | 4 | 7 | 46 |
| Stirling Albion | 31 | 19 | 6 | 6 | 44 |
| St Mirren | 33 | 18 | 7 | 8 | 43 |
| Raith Rovers | 32 | 17 | 8 | 7 | 42 |
| Montrose | 30 | 14 | 8 | 8 | 36 |
| Cowdenbeath | 32 | 14 | 8 | 10 | 36 |
| Hamilton Acas. | 32 | 14 | 6 | 12 | 34 |
| Berwick R. | 32 | 14 | 5 | 13 | 33 |
| Stenhousemuir | 31 | 12 | 7 | 12 | 31 |
| Alloa Athletic | 32 | 9 | 10 | 13 | 28 |
| East Stirling | 34 | 10 | 8 | 16 | 28 |
| Queen's Park | 32 | 8 | 11 | 13 | 27 |
| Queen of South | 31 | 10 | 7 | 14 | 27 |
| Stranraer | 31 | 11 | 3 | 17 | 25 |
| Forfar Athletic | 33 | 8 | 9 | 16 | 25 |
| Clydebank | 31 | 8 | 5 | 18 | 21 |
| Albion Rovers | 33 | 5 | 7 | 21 | 17 |
| Brechin City | 31 | 5 | 3 | 23 | 13 |

## Player Pic – Billy Paterson                    Gordon Sydney

Mention the name Billy Paterson to most Clyde fans who remember this season and I'd bet quite a few will return blank looks. That's because you would have to have been up at Central Park Cowdenbeath between three o'clock and twenty to five on the 7th of April 1973 to see Billy playing his only game for the Bully Wee – he was even listed in some reports as "Newman". Now, if you walked four or five miles along the road from Shawfield and came into Cambuslang you would get a completely different response if you mentioned the name Billy Peterson. Billy, you see, was an integral part of the great Cambuslang Rangers team of the early seventies, and is revered in that part of the world (I'd recommend you take a look at the article covering Billy's career on the SJFA website). So how near did we get to signing Billy? Not very, he tells me – as far as he remembers this was only a short-term loan, to help Archie Robertson out with a depleted squad.

Another one that got away!


## Strange Visitors...

Stranger visitors to the terracing were (maybe) spotted at Cowdenbeath's Central Park ground, as **Brian Ahern** recollects...

*"I'm not sure if it was this game, but I remember the team bus arrived at Central Park, and we walked through and out to the pitch for a wee look about, and I always remember there was a cow on the terracing – it was of course gone by the time we kicked off!"*

| | |
|---|---|
| **DATE** | Saturday 14th April 1973 |
| **TOURNAMENT** | League Division Two |
| **FINAL SCORE** | Clyde 1 Alloa Athletic 0 |
| **TEAM** | *Cairney, Anderson, Swan; Burns, Houston, McGoldrick; Sullivan, Thomson, Millar, McGrain and Ahern Sub McVie* |
| **SCORER(S)** | *Swan* |
| **ATTENDANCE** | 1510 |
| **REPORTER** | Alan Maxwell |

Having only picked up the one point from the previous two Saturday trips away from home, Bully Wee nerves were clearly evident leading into the penultimate home League fixture.

In the lead-up to the game, the main talking point was the long-awaited return in goal by Phil Cairney. It took a fair bit of persuasion from gaffer Archie Robertson though. Phil had been to a specialist the day before the match for a check-up on his injured knee and it looked as though a cartilage operation might be necessary. But once Mr. Robertson and Phil got down to a serious chat, the misunderstanding on his improvement reports was cleared up; Phil agreed to turn out against the Wasps.

Talking of goalkeepers, our opponents had between the sticks Dave McWilliams, who would end up playing for Clyde in the early-eighties.

In the eighth minute Phil Cairney punched clear, and Dom Sullivan picked up the loose ball. He ran half the length of the pitch, but his shot was saved by McWilliams down at his post. A minute later a great move involving Sam Millar, Danny McGrain and Colin Thomson let the latter in for a shot, but once again McWilliams was equal to the task, brilliantly pushing his shot over the bar.

Sadly, the tension took over after this early burst, and Clyde were unable to produce the natural, calm footballing ability that had got them to the top of the tree. It made for a frustrating afternoon, eased only by an eighty–third minute goal from Aldo Swan that secured the points….and our immediate return to the top Division.

There will need to be a vast improvement in our shooting ability if that return is to prove fruitful. Clyde had chance after chance to open the scoring, and whilst great credit should go to Dave McWilliams in the visitors' goal, the Bully Wee forwards will require to regain some of their earlier season composure in front of goal.

For all their superiority, the return of Cairney in goal was to prove game changing on two separate occasions when he pulled off a couple of tremendous saves at vital times, when the game remained scoreless.

And so, promotion clinched; bring on the Championship Title with just two games remaining!

## Player Pic – Alan Swan                    Alan Maxwell

An Electrician to trade, Alan Swan signed for Clyde in January 1970, from Shettleston Juniors. Originally signed as a forward, he switched successfully to full back with the Bully Wee and made the left back position his own following the departure of his mentor, the inimitable Eddie Mulheron, to South Africa.

Alan made 37 appearances for the Bully Wee in season 1972/73, scoring 3 goals and establishing a rock-solid partnership with Eddie Anderson. Indeed, the

pair together were described as the best young full back partnership in Scotland by fellow player Billy Beattie, and I for one am not about to dispute the point! Defensively sound, Alan never forgot his roots as a forward and he flourished this season under Archie Robertson's leadership. The Manager encouraged both his full backs to utilise their attacking flair and get forward at every opportunity and this helped not only add to the potency of Clyde as an attacking force but also curtailed opposition wingers who had to spend much of their time chasing back to cover the overlapping runs of Swan and his partner.

Alan was a bit of a joker in the dressing room, a fact attested to in later years by another Clyde hero of the 70's, Neil Hood. He may have picked up some of this from working with Eddie Mulheron in his early years with Clyde. Alan described training with Mulheron as *"...one big series of gags.....we got through the work but Eddie helped it go with a laugh."*

To cap a tremendous season for Alan personally, he was voted the Supporters Player of the Year. Supporters then were no less forgiving or critical of their heroes than they are today, and this fully deserved award best sums up just what a great season it had been for the hugely popular left back, particularly considering the array of talent that was in the Clyde squad at the time.

| DATE | Saturday 21st April 1973 |
|---|---|
| TOURNAMENT | League Division Two |
| FINAL SCORE | Clydebank 0 Clyde 1 |
| TEAM | *Cairney, Anderson, Swan; Burns, Houston, McGoldrick; Sullivan, Thomson, Millar, McGrain and Harvey Sub Ahern* |
| SCORER(S) | *Millar* |
| ATTENDANCE | 2330 |
| REPORTER | Alan Maxwell |

And so, after 34 gruelling League encounters, the big day had finally arrived.

At last, a chance for the Robertson Babes' to clinch the Title. This was no foregone conclusion; our recent League form had not been overwhelming. Whilst now assured of promotion, the big carrot was the League Championship itself.

Gallagher in the Bankies goal made a good save right at the start; indeed after 10 minutes the home team had still not crossed the half-way line. Colin Thomson picked up a poor Clydebank clearance, his shot looked net bound but it cannoned off a defender and carried high over the crossbar. Clyde kept up the pressure but their finishing was woeful.

They kept pushing however, though three consecutive corner kicks were to prove fruitless. The home team were beginning to participate and Cairney had to look smart to gather a McColl drive to goal. Just on the half-time whistle a free-kick from McCall hit the goalpost and rebounded into play.

Hard as he tried, skipper McGrain couldn't get his midfield colleagues to produce the vital spark. Then Joe McGoldrick was short with a pass back which Cairney only just managed to reach before the in-rushing Mike Larnach. And then, right on the hour mark, the big breakthrough. Sammy Millar picked up a loose ball, and from all of 30 yards rifled a cracking shot past the helpless Gallagher.

Young teenager Bobby Harvey added to his growing reputation with a strong midfield performance, and came very close to scoring. And so, the party began a memorable champagne reception in the tiny Kilbowie changing room…. **CHAMPIONS** at last.

*Celebrations in the Kilbowie Dressing Room*

The league table after that match against Clydebank looked like this. Early season pacesetters Cowdenbeath and Stirling Albion had both fallen away to varying degrees, and Dunfermline Athletic, who had come down with Clyde around a year ago, had confirmed their promotion back to the First Division.

| | P | W | D | L | Pts |
|---|---|---|---|---|---|
| **Clyde** | **35** | **22** | **10** | **3** | **54** |
| Dunfermline | 35 | 23 | 5 | 7 | 51 |
| St Mirren | 35 | 19 | 9 | 7 | 45 |
| Stirling Albion | 35 | 19 | 8 | 8 | 45 |
| Raith Rovers | 35 | 18 | 9 | 8 | 45 |
| Montrose | 35 | 18 | 8 | 9 | 44 |
| Cowdenbeath | 35 | 14 | 9 | 12 | 37 |
| Hamilton Acas. | 35 | 15 | 6 | 14 | 36 |
| Berwick R. | 35 | 15 | 5 | 15 | 35 |
| Stenhousemuir | 35 | 13 | 8 | 14 | 34 |
| Alloa Athletic | 35 | 11 | 10 | 14 | 32 |
| Queen of South | 34 | 12 | 8 | 14 | 32 |
| East Stirling | 36 | 12 | 8 | 16 | 32 |
| Queen's Park | 35 | 9 | 11 | 15 | 29 |
| Forfar Athletic | 35 | 10 | 9 | 16 | 29 |
| Stranraer | 35 | 13 | 3 | 19 | 29 |
| Clydebank | 35 | 9 | 5 | 21 | 23 |

## Player Pic – Sam Millar                Graeme Clark

Sam Millar joined the Clyde in 1970 from St Luke's Boys Guild, the same team as Brian Ahern, and made his name, no more so than in this season, as a strong, bustling centre forward. Described by his captain Danny McGrain, as "the iron man of the team", he made a huge contribution to the success of the season, scoring 11 goals in 42 starts (out of a possible 44).

At just 19, Sam formed a fearsome strike force with Peter Boyle, and was the ideal man to play alongside Boyle. It's fair to say that Millar had to play second fiddle to Boyle in the press notices but that should not detract from the amount of invaluable work done during the season by student Millar. He was willing to take endless punishment from opposing defenders and never let up himself, his endless probing causing all sorts of difficulties for the opposition. There can be no greater compliment to Sam Millar than his name being one of the first on the team sheet each week.

And Sam, of course, grabbed the single vital goal that won us the Championship this season – and right in front of the TV camera's – when he fired home from distance against Clydebank at Kilbowie Park.

Sam's footballing ability was such that he could play in a variety of roles, and latterly in his Clyde career he filled the right-half position following Danny McGrain's injury.

| | |
|---|---|
| **DATE** | Saturday 28th April 1973 |
| **TOURNAMENT** | League Division Two |
| **FINAL SCORE** | Clyde 5 St Mirren 1 |
| **TEAM** | *Cairney, Anderson, Swan; Burns, McVie, McGoldrick;* |
| | *Sullivan, Millar, Thomson, McGrain and Ahern Sub* |
| | *McHugh (for McVie)* |
| **SCORER(S)** | *Millar (2), Thomson (2), Sullivan* |
| **ATTENDANCE** | 1449 |
| **REPORTER** | Jim Hutchison |

# "HAIL THE BULLY WEE CHAMPIONS!"

So read one headline after the previous weeks' match at Kilbowie where the title was clinched, and it was party time on the terraces of Shawfield, with the 1500 fans in fine voice for this the last game of the season.

What a contrast to the previous season when we were relegated in the corresponding last day fixture and a lasting memory was of Danny McGrain being led off the field in tears.

Now Scottish Football's smallest captain must have felt he was ten-foot-tall as he led Clyde back into the First Division as Champions in a single season!

With the pressure off and the title "in the bag" the Bully Wee finished off their season in some style by thumping the Paisley Saints.

Sam Millar picked up where he had left off the previous Saturday by opening the scoring in 22 minutes with a neat header.

Colin Thompson added number two 15 minutes later after Millar slipped him through and he lashed it past the helpless Stevenson in the visiting goal.

Clyde passed up a number of good chances to extend their lead before half time against what was in truth a poor Saints side, playing only for their pride.

Clyde's third goal was a thing of real beauty that will live long in the memory. A neat passing move ended with a Brian Ahern cross being only partially cleared and the advancing Dom Sullivan met the ball and volleyed a left footed screamer into the net in 57 minutes.

Five minutes later Sam Millar struck again to make it 4-0 and send the crowd into raptures.

John Dickson of St. Mirren did score what could by then only be considered a consolation goal in the 79th minute.

Clyde weren't finished though and Colin Thomson got his second and Clyde's fifth in the 83rd minute to round off a very impressive display as we signed off from Second Division football.

St. Mirren were looking to the referee to blow the final whistle by the end of a dismal day for them and Archie Robertson declared he was delighted but felt we could have won by an even greater margin. Remarks which emphasised the difference between the two sides on the day.

A sad footnote was that two goal Colin Thompson and Eddie McGuinness were the only two players released immediately after the match as Clyde prepared for life in the First Division.

At least it was not as brutal a cull of playing staff that had shocked the fans after relegation the previous season and Clyde would strengthen for the next season, but that is a story for another day.

*Final score...Willie McVie 6 Danny McGrain 2...*

## The Final League Table...

Makes good reading!

First to lead the league were Cowdenbeath, then Stirling Albion took over and set a fair pace for a few months. After the Ne'erday match at Hampden Clyde went to the top and stayed there. We might not have scored the goals that other teams managed, but our points total beat every other team, and that's what matters!

|                  | P  | W  | D  | L  | F  | A  | Pts |
|------------------|----|----|----|----|----|----|-----|
| Clyde            | 36 | 23 | 10 | 3  | 68 | 28 | 56  |
| Dunfermline Ath  | 36 | 23 | 6  | 7  | 95 | 32 | 52  |
| Raith Rovers     | 36 | 19 | 9  | 8  | 73 | 39 | 47  |
| Stirling Albion  | 36 | 19 | 9  | 8  | 70 | 42 | 47  |
| St Mirren        | 36 | 19 | 7  | 10 | 79 | 50 | 45  |
| Montrose         | 36 | 18 | 8  | 10 | 82 | 58 | 44  |
| Cowdenbeath      | 36 | 14 | 10 | 12 | 57 | 53 | 38  |
| Hamilton         | 36 | 16 | 6  | 14 | 67 | 63 | 38  |
| Berwick Rangers  | 36 | 16 | 6  | 15 | 45 | 54 | 37  |
| Stenhousemuir    | 36 | 14 | 8  | 14 | 44 | 41 | 36  |
| Queen of the Sth | 36 | 13 | 8  | 15 | 45 | 52 | 34  |
| Alloa Ath        | 36 | 11 | 11 | 14 | 45 | 49 | 33  |
| East Stirling    | 36 | 12 | 8  | 16 | 52 | 69 | 32  |
| Queens Park      | 36 | 9  | 12 | 15 | 44 | 61 | 30  |
| Stranraer        | 36 | 13 | 4  | 19 | 56 | 78 | 30  |
| Forfar Ath       | 36 | 10 | 9  | 17 | 38 | 66 | 29  |
| Clydebank        | 36 | 9  | 6  | 21 | 48 | 72 | 24  |
| Albion Rovers    | 36 | 5  | 8  | 23 | 35 | 83 | 18  |
| Brechin City     | 36 | 5  | 4  | 27 | 46 | 99 | 14  |

## Manager Profile – Archie Robertson                    Gordon Sydney

The team performed on the park, the results put us top of the table, and steering us through the entire season was manager Archie Robertson. Archie, by all accounts, was a studious, scientific manager, who would employ methods such as getting the players in the car park at Shawfield practicing their passing skills and ball control for hours on end.

The respect, admiration and appreciation shown by all who played under Archie still lives on to this day – I can clearly remember Dom Sullivan praising Archie in his speech after Brian Ahern came into the Hall of Fame – Brian done likewise – and these two aren't unique by any means.

Archie came back from Cowdenbeath to manage Clyde in January 1968, and he had a major rebuilding task to undertake. The Class of '67, who had taken Clyde to third place in Scotland, just behind the European Champions and The Cup Winners Cup runners-up, and a Scottish Cup semi-final, was splitting up, with players moving on. Simultaneously, with Celtic winning the European Cup (and almost everything else they competed for around that time), and people being decamped from Glasgow City out to the new towns, crowds were dwindling. It was already a very difficult task for Archie to maintain or better the success of '67, without adding in these factors (and probably many others as well).

After relegation in April 1972 the decision was taken to focus on finding, nurturing and developing young players, hence we were treated to the "Robertson's Babes" this season.

I hope you'll forgive me for not writing a new article here, but on the following pages I have reproduced an article written some years ago by Jim Hutchison – it seemed the most appropriate of articles to reproduce here.

# ARCHIE ROBERTSON; CLYDE'S CLASSIEST EVER?

## Jim Hutchison

In this day and age where TV Pundits trot out cliché after cliché branding some grossly overpaid Premier Star as the next big thing, it is comforting to look back at the real stars of the past that were paid a fraction of the modern player's salary's but outclassed their modern contemporary by the proverbial country mile.

Such a football artist was Archie Robertson, another shining star of the Clyde sides of the 1950's, who along with Tommy Ring, is well worthy of the title of Clyde Legend.

Sadly, like so many in the stands these days I never had the pleasure of witnessing the class and finesse of an exceptionally skilful player in action but have been regaled many times (*usually by Jimmy Morrison!*) with stories of a man who truly graced the Shawfield turf during the club's halcyon days of the fifties.

So, what is offered here can do little justice to his glittering career which in many ways closely mirrored that of Tommy Ring when during their playing careers Clyde landed two Scottish Cups and also played and won the same lower division honours as Tommy but he did suffer a further relegation in 1961, with Tommy having departed to Everton by that time.

Archie made his Scotland debut in a 3-0 win over Portugal in 1995 – playing alongside Tommy Ring – and made four further international appearances, scoring the opener in a 4-1 win in Austria in 1955 and also grabbing the first goal in the 3-2 World Cup qualifying victory against Switzerland at Hampden in November 1957. His final appearance for Scotland was at the 1958 World Cup Finals in Sweden when he played in the 3-2 defeat by Paraguay. He can also count having played twice for the Scottish League.

There is a difference of opinions over Archie Robertson's early career details where one source indicates him playing for Eastwood Academy before joining Clyde shortly before his 18th birthday in 1947 while another agrees he joined in

1947 but from junior side Rutherglen Glencairn, the latter option is what my own understanding was where Archie joined from. Either way we can agree that he made his Clyde debut in 1949-50 and stayed on the Shawfield payroll as a player until 1961.

His career details with Clyde were: 293 League appearances (twice an ever-present) and 121 goals, 60 League Cup appearances amassing 33 goals, 37 Scottish Cup appearances scoring 17 goals, including that never to be forgotten equaliser direct from the corner against Celtic in the first match in 1955. Arguably Clyde's most important goal as it gave the club what seemed at the time a forlorn hope of a second bite at the Cup, which of course history tells us we won 1-0. He also made eight other first class appearances for Clyde, scoring four goals. Not a bad scoring record from an inside forward or midfield player in modern parlance!

The season's most dramatic goal. The scene in the Celtic goal in the last minutes of the Scottish Cup Final as Robertson scores Clyde's equalizing goal from a corner

In the summer of 1961 Archie's playing career ended with the Bully Wee and he moved to Morton for a fee of £1,000 where he made a further 51 League appearances, scoring 18 goals. He also made 11 League Cup appearances for the Cappielow club, scoring once and played in one Scottish Cup tie. He was eventually freed by Morton at the end of 1963-64 season and he moved on to Cowdenbeath, initially as player-manager, but hung up his boots after five further League appearances brought three more goals.

He continued as Cowdenbeath manager until 1967 when he returned back to Shawfield to take over as Clyde boss in 1968, where his managerial career replicated his playing days with Clyde, with relegation in 1972 duly be followed by an immediate return to top flight football the next season as Champions.

Archie left Shawfield in 1973, and later became a scout for Tottenham Hotspur.

It was only a mere five years later in 1978 that sadly Archie Robertson died at the ridiculously early age of just 48, how I would have loved to talk to him now and find out about all those happier times when Clyde were flying high at the very top of Scottish football.

## Memories...

When the idea of the book moved into reality, albeit about two years ago now, I asked supporters to send me in their recollections of the season. Some of these I have weaved into the fabric of the book in (hopefully) appropriate places, but for two in particular it seemed better to keep them together, to be reproduced here in their entirety...

**Paul Reid** kicks it off...

"My abiding memory [of 72/73] is the final match of the season when we thrashed St Mirren 5- 1 at Shawfield. I remember 'Congratulations' by Cliff Richard being played before the game, in celebration of us winning the league the previous week with a 1-0 victory at Kilbowie against Clydebank. Sam Millar the scorer before he retired from football to concentrate on his studies.

At this game, and many others, youngsters would sit on the white wall with their legs dangling towards the side of the pitch. The police would walk round time and time again to tell them to sit the other way but as soon as the policeman moved off the legs would be over again. Petty law enforcement. And of course, during this season and many others, fathers would lift sons over the turnstiles in order for them to get free entry. A host of youngsters would wait by the turnstiles and ask for a lift over from an adult.

Great players that season including Dom Sullivan who amazingly got regular abuse from Clyde fans who failed to recognise his undoubted talent. I remember my father, a great admirer of Sullivan, almost coming to blows with another fan who criticised him for his positive comments regarding Sullivan's play. My father was met with the question, 'you'll be here to see that prima donna I suppose'. Poetic timing a minute or so later when Sullivan placed a lovely cross that resulted in a goal.

Peter Boyle? What a striker and Danny McGrain a fearless, committed player who quite literally put his life on the line for the Club when he cleared a Dundee United shot off the line a season or so later. I remember when Danny came back to the club for an award after his injury and walked across the pitch in his suit towards the terracing and got a tremendous ovation. A tear in my eye and a lump in my throat watching him do a little jig in front of the supporters.

130

All-in-all a great set of players managed by a man ahead of his time and club legend Archie Robertson.

Finally, a couple of noteworthy supporters including Angus from East Kilbride. What a voice and always pessimistic about our prospects. Another man who used to berate opposition players by describing them as 'Chanty Wrastlers'. Priceless.

Great days and memories that will live forever."


And **Andy Fleming** continues…

"Season 72/73, where do you start with so many heroes and memories from that season?

Phil Cairney…. I liked Phil's goalkeeping style, and still think the performance he put in at Shawfield against Ayr United was the best goalkeeping display I have ever seen (a season or two after we were promoted).

The Joe McGoldrick / Willie McVie partnership that struck fear into any opposition forwards. Especially man mountain McVie. Nothing silky there but very effective in breaking up opposition attacks.

Alan Swan…a very fine and skilled left back who could turn defence into attack.

Brian 'Fishy' Ahern….class personified with a left foot that could perform magic.

Dom Sullivan…the most skilled of them all who could make a fool of many opponents at will.

Peter Boyle….every goalkeeper's nightmare who never stopped harassing opponents and scored lots of excellent goals.

Lastly but not least our youngest ever captain at 19 years, Danny McGrain. I first saw Danny winning the Scottish Junior Cup at Ibrox with Blantyre Vics, and his work-rate was phenomenal. What he lacked in inches he made up for in heart, and he would cover every inch of grass during a game.

Unfortunately, his career was cut short by a head injury, and I can still see him stopping a fierce shot from one of Dundee United's players by heading it off the line in a match at Shawfield. Later we heard he had collapsed in the dressing room after the game.

Despite trying to make a comeback he was forced to retire, and who knows what heights he would have reached in the game. My own personal nickname for him was Little-Big-Man and that he was.

These were my personal favourites but all the players of that season played a big part in getting us promoted."

## I Thank You...

Of course, my thanks go out to many people for their involvement with this book, starting with my friends, fellow authors and Clyde Supporters Alan "Aldo" Maxwell, Jim Hutchison and Graeme "Sharkey" Clark. The effort these guys put in was very much appreciated, as was their patience and understanding. But occasionally things went wrong, for instance when Jim's PC crashed, inspiring "Sharkey" to poetry...

*There was a young Clyde fan called Hutch,*
*Whose PC had left him in the lurch*
*Good money was spent*
*But the stupid thing remained bent*
*And that's why Syd swears so much!*

John Taylor as ever was extremely helpful. His newspaper cuttings saved many hours trawling through old newspapers, and without his photographs this book would be very much worse! NB This had nothing to do with John featuring in a small way in this book- we were not influenced in any way, shape or form!

And there's Fraser Bruce, who took the time out to talk to me and send me an extensive email with the story of the Clyde FC single.

Then there's the fans (aside from the authors) that have contributed to the book (in no particular order) ...David Cunningham, Paul Reid, Tom Kelly and Andy Fleming.

I've included quotes and / or stories extracted from the match programme of the time – John and Craig Rodger spring to mind in this context - I hope you don't mind me including these without contacting you!

Craig Black is currently our match photographer, who quietly goes about his voluntary task of producing excellent match photographs, and who is also capable of turning ordinary scans from old programmes into wonderful pictures for inclusion in this book. Thanks Craig, a brilliant job done there.

Di, my wife, for being a "Clyde-widow" much of the time I'm at home (this might well apply to some wife's as well)!

And last but certainly not least there's the players, and management staff at the time, without whom we wouldn't be writing (and reading) this book!

Chairman: Willie Dunn

Vice-Chairman: Tom Clark

Directors:
- G Johnstone
- Ian Paterson (Club Treasurer)
- Dr John Crorie
- Billy Dunn
- John Scoullar (deceased), replaced in the course of the season by
- John McBeth

Manager: Archie Robertson

Physio: Lawrie Smith

Trainer: Jim Eadie

Groundsman: Hughie McLellan

The Players: Instead of repeating myself, the full list of players and their "stats" are on the following two pages

## The Statistics – Appearances

| Player | League | League Cup | Scottish Cup | Total |
|---|---|---|---|---|
| Anderson E | 36 | 6 | 2 | 44 |
| McGrain D | 36 | 6 | 2 | 44 |
| Millar S | 34 | 6 | 2 | 42 |
| Houston L | 33 | 6 | 2 | 41 |
| Ahern B | 33 | 6 | 2 | 41 |
| Cairney P | 32 | 6 | 2 | 40 |
| Swan A | 30 | 6 | 1 | 37 |
| Boyle P | 29 | 6 | 2 | 37 |
| Burns Jim | 34 | 0 | 2 | 36 |
| Sullivan D | 30 | 6 | 0 | 36 |
| McGoldrick J | 17 | 1 | 2 | 20 |
| McVie W | 12 | 5 | 0 | 17 |
| McGuiness E | 8 | 5 | 0 | 13 |
| Beattie B | 9 | 0 | 1 | 10 |
| McHugh J | 7 | 0 | 2 | 9 |
| Thomson C | 8 | 1 | 0 | 9 |
| Carr N | 4 | 0 | 0 | 4 |
| Harvey B | 2 | 0 | 0 | 2 |
| Hulston B | 1 | 0 | 0 | 1 |
| Paterson B | 1 | 0 | 0 | 1 |

## Notes

1. Substitute "appearances" aren't complete, so aren't reflected in the table above.
2. The match programme lists Jim Burns first appearance of the season as coming against Queen of the South, however several other records show Jim as having played the game before, against Forfar. I have opted for the latter approach, and this is reflected in the Stats above.

# The Statistics – Goals

| Player | League | League Cup | Scottish Cup | Total |
|--------|--------|------------|--------------|-------|
| **Boyle P** | **14** | 2 | 0 | 16 |
| **Millar S** | 9 | 1 | 1 | 11 |
| **Ahern B** | 9 | 0 | 1 | 10 |
| **Sullivan D** | 7 | **3** | 0 | 10 |
| **McVie W** | 5 | 1 | 0 | 6 |
| **Houston L** | 5 | 0 | 0 | 5 |
| **Beattie B** | 4 | 0 | 0 | 4 |
| **Thomson C** | 3 | 0 | 1 | 4 |
| **Swan A** | 2 | 1 | 0 | 3 |
| **McGrain D** | 2 | 0 | 0 | 2 |
| **McGuiness E** | 1 | 1 | 0 | 2 |
| **Hulston B** | 2 | 0 | 0 | 2 |
| **Anderson E** | 1 | 0 | 0 | 1 |
| **Burns Jim** | 1 | 0 | 0 | 1 |
| **Harvey B** | 1 | 0 | 0 | 1 |

## Notes

1. We "benefitted" to the tune of two "own goals" this season.

2. The match programme shows Billy Beattie and Colin Thomson scoring against Berwick Rangers at the end of September, however some contemporary reports indicate Billy Beattie scored twice in that game. Having discussed matters, we have elected to go with the match programme and credit one of those goals to Colin Thomson.

## From Tears to Cheers…

And so the season ended successfully. Where in April 1972 we had tasted the bitterness of relegation, in April 1973 we tasted only success, firstly promotion then the Second Division Championship.

Along the way we had assembled a great young team, under the leadership of Archie Robertson, a man ahead of his time in terms of his coaching philosophies, and a man who tried his best to transfer his skills and learnings to a new generation of young footballers.

Danny McGrain was one of that generation of younger players. Touted regularly as a player that would go on to play at a higher level, his "tears" at our relegation were turned into "cheers" with our return to the First Division. Sadly, his football career and ultimately his life were ended far too soon, but Danny's story and memory inspired Jim Hutchison to suggest the title of the book.

*What a difference a year makes – Danny McGrain goes "From Tears to Cheers…"*

NB One thing Danny didn't win was that bet with Willie McVie to see who would score the most goals! Willie's move to a more forward role certainly benefitted him, and he ran out winner by six goals to two, but Danny didn't complain, he simply got on with it.

Finally, amongst my "Thank You" notes I used a small verse by Graeme "Sharkey" Clark. Graeme, though, isn't the only supporter to be inspired to write poetry. Tom Kelly's poem on the following pages, simply entitled **72/73**, seems an appropriate way to end this book…

# 72/73 by Tom Kelly

This poem is about winning the promotion race,
After a season where we fell from grace!
Supporting a team with energy to burn,
Making sure of a quick return!

At the end of the season in '73,
"Dawn" tied a ribbon round the "Old Oak Tree",
Ajax won the European Cup,
As for Clyde, the only way was UP!

Now forty-odd years takes me back in time,
When my spoken word didn't come in rhyme.
So, bear with me as I try to look back,
At the Clyde team, from defence to attack.

Phil Cairney in goal, was a regular to play,
Shoulder-length hair, young man going grey.
Anderson, Beattie and Alan Swan,
Solid defenders you could rely on.

Today they're called midfielders, back then it was half-back,
Moving the ball from defence to attack,
Ahern, McVie, not forgetting John McHugh,
Getting a full cap, he was at the end of the queue!

Danny McGrain deserves a verse of his own,
In many a game he stood out alone.
A life cut short at an early age,
For a player who commanded centre-stage!

Dom Sullivan and Bobby Harvey, wingers of note,
Caught many defenders on the "stoat".
As for goalscorers, all could toil,
But none were better than Peter Boyle.

McGuinness, McGoldrick and Sam Millar,
Colin Thomson, Liam Houston and many another,
Neil Carr, Billy Hulston and Jimmy Burns,
All these players gave us good turns.

Archie Robertson, remember the name
He was the player of corner kick fame.
Straight from a corner late in the game,
Against the Celtic – instant Fame!

Some managers gave us lots to regret,
But Archie Robertson we won't forget.

\*\*\*\*\*\*\*\*\*\*\*\*\*\*\*\*\*\*\*\*\*\*\*\*\*\*\*\*\*\*\*\*\*\*\*\*\*\*\*\*\*\*\*\*\*\*\*\*\*\*\*\*\*\*\*\*

L - #0294 - 271118 - C0 - 210/148/7 - PB - DID2374610